Roundtable

Erratum

On the cover,
Father Moore's name
should read:
Gareth Moore, O.P.

Roundtable

Conversations with
European Theologians

Michael Bauman

BAKER BOOK HOUSE
Grand Rapids, Michigan 49516

Copyright 1990 by
Baker Book House Company

Printed in the United States of America

Library of Congress Cataloging-in-Publication Data
Bauman, Michael.
    Roundtable : conversations with European theologians / Michael
Bauman.
        p.   cm.
    Includes index.
    ISBN 0-8010-0986-3
    1. Theologians—Europe—Interviews.   2. Theology—20th Century.
I. Title.
    BR50.B37 1990
230'.094—dc20   90-40149
                                                CIP

For
John Reist
and
Robert Umidi,

who know both the beauty of faith
and the challenge of theology

Contents

Preface

When, in 1638, John Milton left his father's house at Horton for Italy, he had a Cambridge University master's degree to his credit and more than four additional years of private study at home. He felt himself ready to undertake what for scholars during the English Renaissance had become the customary capstone of the training of a cultured mind—the continental "grand tour." Such tours were designed to equip those scholars with a working knowledge of European languages other than English, to broaden their cultural horizons by exposing them to the art, traditions, and lifestyles of other nations, and to gain for them a degree of sophistication not readily obtained locally.

Such tours also afforded English Renaissance scholars the opportunity to meet some of the greatest luminaries in their own chosen fields of interest or expertise. Sir Philip Sidney, for instance, met with Peter Ramus, the philosopher; with Henri Estienne, the publisher; with Tintoretto and Veronese, the painters; with Cesare Caraffa, the Italian Protestant; and with Torquato Tasso, the epic poet. Milton himself called on Hugo Grotius, the Dutch Arminian theologian, lawyer, and poet; on Giovanni Diodati, the Calvinist biblical commentator from Geneva; and on Galileo, the persecuted Italian astronomer.

I, too, have taken a European grand tour of sorts, and I have spoken with some of the finest theological scholars in the United Kingdom and on the Continent. They have done their best to answer the questions I posed to them, questions I thought were of the greatest significance.

This book is the fruit of my international pilgrimage in search of the theological wisdom that emancipates the mind from the shackles of its own ignorance and that opens it to beauty, truth, and goodness, wherever they can be found. I have found it in the modest but comfortable homes of an Eastern Orthodox bishop in Oxford and of a Dutch Reformed theologian in Leyden, in the small and cozy upstairs rooms of an Anglican nun, and in the formal and functional third-floor offices of a scholar in Munich.

While Sidney's and Milton's international tours were financed by the happy combination of family fortune and parental largesse, I owe my European pilgrimage to Clifford Knight, a devout Christian benefactor whose generous gifts to the Christian Studies program at Hillsdale College have made possible not only this journey, but my job as well. His contribution to the cause of Christ will always evoke my sincerest gratitude. I acknowledge his generosity here with pleasure.

I credit Cyril David Quatrone, a former student, with the idea for this theological expedition. While reading a prominent American evangelical theologian's memoirs of his meetings in Europe with Karl Barth, Emil Brunner, and Rudolf Bultmann, Cyril complained to me that in what could have been the most intriguing chapter he had read in any theological text, he found only vast amounts of information about European weather and souvenirs. The book contained little information about what those prominent thinkers actually said to one another. I heartily agreed with him that someone should compile such a useful and interesting collection of theological insights and commentary. I intended to discover what contribution I could make. This book, I hope, is a not unworthy response to that intention.

I also want to acknowledge the hospitality and stimulation afforded me by the capable staff of the Centre for Medieval and Renaissance Studies in Oxford, which was my headquarters for the many weeks I spent creating these interviews, and especially John Feneley, the Centre's congenial, energetic, and widely informed principal.

Further, I wish to thank Marsha Boehmke, whose remarkable efficiency produced the complex web of arrangements necessary to make these interviews possible, and who helped ready the manuscript for publication. Catherine Wilson, of the Oxford Summer School in Religious Studies, kindly assisted me in contacting several of the theologians whose insightful comments constitute this book. For her help I am grateful.

I also am grateful to my wife, Sharon, for graciously agreeing to face alone whatever difficulties or crises arose in my absence, and for undertaking all the jobs at home, both large and small, that needed to be done while I, for weeks, was more than an ocean away.

Introduction

Like all other groups of theologians, we evangelicals tend to be insular. We are far more likely to read the works of authors and publishers we know and trust than the works of those whom we do not recognize or from whom we dissent. We do so for a number of reasons, not least because time and energy both are in limited supply and we therefore are unable to read everything we could or should. Furthermore, as fallen beings ourselves, we theologians tend to avoid being disturbed. We do not relish struggling with the ideas of those who call into question the very notions that undergird our theological existence. (Nor do they.) This is simply a case of theological inertia: a body of theologians at rest will tend to stay at rest until moved by an outside force—and who would not rather rest than sweat?

I do not object to the tried and the true. Nor do I counsel anyone to hold them lightly. But if we feed only on versions happening to be in favor with our own small coterie of evangelical theologians, we doubtless shall miss a great deal that would have made us better thinkers, better theologians, indeed better people. The first object of this book, therefore, is to bring to my colleagues within the American evangelical community of scholars the insights and wisdom of those European thinkers whose work normally falls outside the orbit of our daily attention.

My second purpose is to draw theology and theologians back to earth, and here I am not referring only to evangelicals. Theologians of every stripe and hue seem to suffer from the malady of acute impracticality. Our theology seems to rise quickly through the stratosphere, utterly disconnected from the workaday existence of the majority of our fellow citizens in the Western world, and even further away from the benighted and deprived existence of so many of those inhabiting the rest of the globe. Because we tend to ask not only the wrong questions, but the right questions in the wrong way, all too often the gap between theological speculation and practical wisdom is not merely a gap, but a chasm. Therefore, I not only have addressed myself to some of Europe's best theologians, but also have tried to ask questions that count, questions to which the wisest Christians of every age have sought the answers. I have asked them such questions as:

What is a good life, and what good is life?

What is a good death, and what good is death?

What things have made you doubt, and how have you handled them?

Do you have any regrets?

How would you describe God?

What is a human being?

What is the most perfect creed the church has ever written, and why do you think so?

What are you proudest of, or what has given you the most satisfaction?

If you could ask any theologian of any time or place just one question, whom would you ask and what would you ask?

I sought out the theologians I did because I thought I recognized in them the unmistakable marks of having lived a truly theological existence. They struggled, in some cases for decades, to bring the Christian gospel and its manifold implications to bear upon all that we think or do, whether individually or corporately. While I occasionally found myself dissenting, sometimes even sharply, from what they wrote, I knew that theirs was not a theology untouched by human life; nor was theirs (so far as I could tell) a life untouched by theology, itself a distinctly human endeavor. If wisdom were to be gained, I was persuaded that if anyone could provide it these Christian thinkers could.

I sought them out in order to ask them questions about Christian wisdom and to gather for myself some of their insight gleaned from years of scholarly and pious reflection upon the revelation of God in Christ. They had purchased this insight through hard work amid the anguish and the poignant beauty of a fallen world, a world they had seen colored by joy and success and darkened by the shadows of one, sometimes two, world wars. I sought them out because I realize that my own two eyes are not adequate to take in all I might need for a prosperous or productive lifelong theological pilgrimage. I wanted to see through their eyes too.

These theologians proved to be not only a wise assembly of counselors but a diverse one as well. The men and women with whom I spoke were Dutch, German, English, and Scottish; they were Anglican, Reformed, Lutheran, Orthodox, and Roman Catholic; they were laymen, nuns, priests, pastors, bishops, and professors; and they ranged from early career to long retired. These theologians are proof that we evangelicals have much to learn from those who do not share our own theological idiosyncrasies, but who love God, who are used by God, and who are taught by God nevertheless. I am honored to think that, in Christ, each one of these Christians is not only my teacher, guide, and fellow pilgrim, but also my brother or sister. May they prosper.

So may you.

1

Bishop Kallistos (Timothy) Ware
Oxford, England

Bishop Kallistos Ware was born in Bath, England, in 1934 and was educated at Westminster School, London, and Magdalen College, Oxford, where he studied classical languages, philosophy, and theology. Received into the Orthodox Church in 1958, he was ordained priest in 1966, and in the same year took monastic vows at the Monastery of St. John the Theologian in Patmos. Since 1966 he has been lecturer in Eastern Orthodox Studies at the University of Oxford, and in 1970 he became a Fellow of Pembroke College, Oxford. In 1982 he was consecrated Bishop of Diokleia and appointed assistant bishop in the Orthodox Archdiocese of Thyateira and Great Britain. Bishop Kallistos is co-editor of *Sobornost,* the journal of the Fellowship of Saint Alban and Saint Sergius.

Select Bibliography

Eustratios Argenti: A Study of the Greek Church under Turkish Rule. Oxford: Clarendon, 1974.

The Philokalia. 2 vols. Winchester, Mass.: Faber and Faber, 1983.

The Orthodox Church. New York: Penguin, 1984.

The Orthodox Way. Crestwood, N.Y.: Saint Vladimir's Seminary Press, 1986.

The Power of the Name: The Jesus Prayer in Orthodox Spirituality. Oxford: SLG, 1986.

What is a human being?

The essential and distinctive element in a human being is summed up in the biblical phrase, "in the image and likeness of God." That means that we cannot understand the human apart from the divine. We cannot understand the human being alone: we can only understand the human being in relationship with God. We humans have the divine as the determining influence in our person.

All that we say about God, therefore, should also illuminate our understanding of what it is to be human. For example, in that God himself is communal, is a community, indeed is a Trinity, we come to understand that we humans are not complete when we are in isolation, for we are communal too. I need you in order to be myself. Personhood entails relationships. To be human is to be in communion with other human beings after the image of the Trinity.

We human beings, then, have a double orientation: one in relationship to the God in whose image we are, and the other in relationship to other persons because we are in the image of God, *who is Trinity.*

Describe God.

God, for me, is, above all, Trinity.

Here I think of what Saint Gregory of Nazianzus says: "When I speak of God, I mean Father, Son, and Holy Spirit." God, therefore, is not primarily an abstraction—not just primordial being or the unmoved mover.

He is personal. And he's not just one person, but three persons. He is communal. He is a community of persons that love one another. So, I would start from the understanding of God as interpersonal love.

True love is not self-love, it is exchange, reciprocity, solidarity. Such is the way in which we are to understand divine love as well as human.

I deeply regret the way in which the Trinity is passed over in so much Christian thinking today. Karl Rahner rightly observed that one could remove the references to the Trinity from most contemporary books of Christian theology and their arguments would remain unaltered. All too many Christians today are simply monotheists, not trinitarians. One of the most important tasks of the Orthodox Church in the inter-Christian dialogue of our time is to stress the centrality of the doctrine of the Trinity, not as a piece of abstract speculation, but as an expression of practical theology that can make a huge difference to you and me personally. In all our struggles for human rights, for justice, for the abolition of oppression, we are active in the name of the Trinity!

What is the role of the theologian in the church and in the university?

Here I take my cue from the fourth-century desert father Evagrius: "The theologian is the one who prays; and if you pray truly, you are a theologian." Because theology is bound up in this way with personal experience and with prayer, the true theologians are the saints. Theology, therefore, is not primarily an academic discipline. Theology is *not* a science.

Theology, in the true and full sense of the prayerful

vision of God, is clearly something that lies outside the scope of a secular university. But there are certain things that we can do within a university. We can study rigorously what people in the past have said and thought.

So the academic study of theology in a modern secular university needs to be primarily historical in approach, closely linked to the assessment of textual evidence from the past; or else it can be philosophical, an intellectual analysis of the meaning and interconnection of religious concepts. But I doubt whether academic theology can be mandatory, in the sense of telling the student what he or she should believe. We provide him or her with the historical and intellectual tools by which to assess specific expressions of religious belief in the past or the present. But the decision what to believe—and whether to believe at all—has to be made by each one on the basis of his or her own personal experience and prayer.

What things have made you doubt, and how have you handled them?

When I doubt, I tend to doubt in an all-embracing way. I don't doubt particular doctrines; I doubt everything. I ask myself the large "what if" questions: "What if there's nothing at all beyond the material world?" "What if belief in God is nothing but an immense and tragic error?"

If God exists, then the only God in whom I can believe is a God who has become totally human, who has shared in all the fullness of human life and death. So, for me, to believe in God is to be a Christian. And if I am to be a Christian, that means for me an Orthodox Christian, a member of the Orthodox Church. But everything depends on the first step: Does God exist? What do I mean by "God"?

I have learned that when I face such all-embracing doubts, the most effective response is action rather than cerebral argument. Faith returns where I seek to serve and help others. (Perhaps that is so because much of what makes us doubt is not really intellectual but spiritual.)

It also helps me to remember that doubt is one of the inevitable spiritual growing pains. Doubt can sometimes be purely negative, but much more frequently it fulfills a positive function. "Unless a grain of wheat falls into the earth and dies . . .": my false certainties have to be called in question and to die, so that genuine faith may come into being. Doubt is often a sign, not that a person's faith is weak, but that it is alive and growing.

What is the Christian gospel, and what is the most effective way to present it or defend it in the modern world?

The Christian gospel is summed up in the reply given by Peter to our Lord on the road to Caesarea Philippi: "You are the Christ, the Son of the living God" (Matt. 16:16). Essentially, the gospel is to bear witness to Christ as Son of God and as Savior—Son of the Father, present with us through the Holy Spirit. That, to me, is the Good News.

More precisely, the gospel is that, in Christ, God has become human. He has united himself with his creatures in the closest of all possible unions. Christ is not only our creator, he is our brother.

The gospel also entails the crucifixion and the resurrection. Christ has died on the cross for our sins, and has risen from the dead for our justification. In this respect, I view the crucifixion and the resurrection as a single event in an undivided drama.

Incarnation, crucifixion, and resurrection: that is the gospel. That is the Good News.

How can we best bear witness to it?

It is not the way of the Orthodox Church to engage in large evangelistic campaigns, though perhaps we should do so more. I respect the work of someone like Billy

Graham. . . . But, having said that, let me add that I believe the best way to spread Christian faith in our own day is through personal contact, one to one, person to person. In the early church, after the episodes recorded for us in the Book of Acts, there was little open preaching to large crowds. Christianity was spread by a quality of life that attracted outsiders and drew them in; it was spread by a witness that was as often silent as it was spoken. Others were converted not so much by what Christians *said* as by what they *were.* This meant, of course, that everyone was a missionary. We need the same kind of mission today: a mission through personal sanctification and inner prayer.

What aspect of your thought do theologians continue to misunderstand?

To use the phrase of a great Russian theologian of this century, Father Georges Florovsky, theology for me means a "neo-patristic synthesis." I take as my guides the Fathers, especially the Greek fathers. I believe that they speak to our own age, and that we must treat them, not as voices from the distant past, but as contemporary witnesses. This has led others to tell me that I think and write as if the Enlightenment had never occurred. It is a criticism often made of the Orthodox Church in general—a criticism that, in common with other Orthodox, I too need to take seriously. But I continue to regard the Fathers as the surest guides for our present age, the wisest interpreters of the Holy Scripture.

Do you have any regrets?

I do have my regrets, yes indeed. Let me mention just one: In some respects I regret that I have chosen a "mixed life," one that includes at the same time monastic vows, university teaching at Oxford, and pastoral work as a parish priest and bishop. This "mixed life" has raised in me not so much a regret as a nagging question:

Have I done the right thing by giving myself to such diverse activities and responsibilities instead of focusing my energy and attetion more fully and effectively on just one? Have I made the mistake of falling between two or even three stools? Should I have been just a monk, or just a lay teacher in a university?

I do not know. But I am sure that my parochial and pastoral duties, while limiting the time I have available to my theological research, also give depth and urgency to that research.

If you could ask any theologian of any time or place just one question, whom would you ask and what would you ask?

I would ask Saint Maximus the Confessor how he understood Christ's words to the Father in Gethsemane: "Not my will but yours be done" (Luke 22:42). I would do so because of my conviction that the human freedom of Christ is utterly essential to our salvation.

What do you consider the church's most perfect creed or confession of faith, and why do you think so?

I am most drawn to the Niceno-Constantinopolitan Creed of 325/381. I am drawn to it, first, because it is communal, conciliar, and ecumenical—a creed that unites East and West; and secondly, because it is eucharistic—a creed which, although not originally written for the Eucharist, has yet been used at eucharistic worship for over fourteen centuries.

I value the Nicene Creed because it says, not just "I believe *that* there is a God," but "I believe *in* one God." It does not state a theory but expresses a personal commitment. (So does the Apostles' Creed; but that is a specifically Western statement, and lacks the universality of the Nicene Creed.)

The Nicene Creed expresses the faith in a form that is both communal and personal—personal, yet not isolated.

What are the greatest problems facing those in your own religious tradition?

The major threat to the Orthodox Church at the moment is not direct attack by atheist governments in the form of anti-Christian propaganda or active persecution, as has happened until recently in Communist countries. (It is still happening in some of them. One should remember that 85 percent of Orthodox Christians live in Communist lands.) No, it is the threat of secularism that we face in the West, and now increasingly in the traditionally Orthodox countries. There has been a startling advance in secularization in the last thirty years, particularly in Greece. Growing material prosperity has led to a widespread falling away from the church.

Orthodoxy stands today at a point of crucial transition. In the past it has formed part of an all-embracing cultural and ethnic identity. It was eventually unthinkable for a Greek or a Serb not to be an Orthodox Christian. But in the future people will be Orthodox, not because of the accident of birth, not automatically and as a matter of instinct, but as the result of personal commitment and conscious choice. The transition will not be easy!

What advice do you have for those outside your religious tradition, especially American evangelicals?

My advice for those outside the Orthodox tradition is this: As Christians, our witness today must be a humble witness, a self-emptying one. An aggressive and triumphalist Christianity is not going to turn the tide of secularism. We must be kenotic. We must be ready to listen.

And yet we must be Christians without compromise. A faith that is attenuated or diluted will not win the world back to Christ.

Neither intransigent zealots nor timid minimalists, but kenotic maximalists: that is our contemporary vocation.

What books and theologians have had the greatest influence upon you?

The first major influence came when I was sixteen. One day in a bookshop Helen Waddell's *The Desert Fathers* caught my attention—I cannot clearly remember why—and I bought it. As I read it, a new world opened up before me: a world in some ways remote, even bizarre, the world of the hermits and ascetics in fourth-century Egypt, and yet a world full of meaning, unexpectedly illuminating for my own personal condition. Here, I felt, was something that I must learn more about when I grew older, that I must somehow make my own, a world austere and yet profoundly compassionate. I still have my copy of the book heavily annotated and underlined.

A few months later, I started to read the novels of Charles Williams. His *Descent into Hell* and *All Hallow's Eve* showed me, in a way I had never appreciated before, the immediacy of the supernatural, the presence of the extraordinary in the midst of the ordinary. His idea of coinherence, of exchanged love, also appealed to me. I was likewise much influenced by the imaginative fiction of C. S. Lewis. Here I think of *Perelandra,* of his retelling of the Psyche myth in *Till We Have Faces* (that is the most moving of all his books), and also by his children's stories.

Then, as a student at Oxford, I read my first work by an Orthodox author: *The Church Is One,* by the nineteenth-century Russian thinker Alexei Khomiakov. This helped me to understand in a new way the true essence of the church as the communion of saints, embracing together the living and the departed, heaven and earth. Other Russian theologians of our own day who influenced me were Vladimir Lossky, author of *The Mystical Theology of the Eastern Church,* and Georges Florovsky (particularly his essay on "The Catholicity of the Church"). I had the happiness of knowing both of them personally. From among the church fathers, I have been shaped by reading

Saint Ignatius of Antioch, who first enabled me to appreciate the link between the Eucharist and the church. Saint Gregory of Nyssa's *Life of Moses* taught me about inner mystical power. I have also gained immensely from Saint Maximus the Confessor, with his remarkable powers of synthesis.

What are the beauties and utilities of your theology, and what are its weaknesses and shortcomings?

I highly value the "total approach" of Orthodox theology. I value its emphasis on the liturgical and the mystical. Any theology, to be complete, must unite doctrine and worship, word and silence.

I value the "apophatic" dimension within Orthodoxy, its insistence upon the radical unknowability of God. This "negative" approach prevents us from making God a mere projection of our own ideas. It reminds us that God is at one and the same time both closer to us than our own hearts, and yet a mystery beyond all understanding. Pascal has said that we need to be simultaneously at two extremities. That is what Orthodoxy at its best succeeds in doing: it bears witness to both the nearness and the otherness of the Divine.

I value Orthodoxy's maximalist view of the incarnation, which teaches that Christ is *completely* God and *completely* man, and that we must not diminish either side.

I value Orthodoxy's affirmative view of material creation, which shows us that we are not saved *from* the world, but *with* the world. In this regard I appreciate Orthodoxy's emphasis upon the transfiguration of Christ and the way it foreshadows the transfiguration of the whole cosmos.

Within Orthodox spirituality, I value above all else "The Jesus Prayer," which I believe very strongly is a prayer for our times: a contemplative prayer, that is yet so simple and so flexible that it can be used by everyone, even in conditions of utmost stress.

On the other side of the coin, however, I find a painful gap between our Orthodox principles and our practice. We have a beautiful theology of the church, a theology of eucharistic catholicity. And yet in practice throughout the Western world, we are culturally fragmented into competing ecclesiastical jurisdictions. We seem simply unable to co-operate as we should. We are divided along nationalistic lines. In the healing of these jurisdictional divisions I detect at the moment no real progress, and for that I grieve day and night.

What is a good life, and what good is life? What is a good death, and what good is death?

A good life is a life lived after the image of the Trinity. It is a life in which I have been able to love other persons. The most important thing in life, the only *real* good, is personal relationships, what Martin Buber called the "I and Thou."

What good is life? I can find meaning in life only if I learn to help others, to share with them the benefits of love. I am called to follow the way of exchange, of substituted love, as Charles Williams used to say. Thus, I look to the Trinity, and when I do, I see mutual love as the most important thing.

What is a good death? We can prepare for death, and indeed we should do so throughout our life. And yet we always approach death "unready and in fear: we cannot go to our death confident in our own righteousness." But at the same time we can pass into the world to come not merely with fear or passive acceptance but with eagerness and expectation, with faith in the risen Christ, in whom there is no more death.

When I think of what good death might be, I recall the desert fathers and how they call us to remember death each day and hour of our life. Such remembrance of death is not somber and morbid. It is not world-denying; it is life-enhancing. Suppose that we went to visit a friend, and knew that this conversation with him would be our last conversation on earth: would we not select our words and our subject matter with the greatest possible care, would we not value every glance and gesture, and treasure it in our memory? "Remember death" means that we live the whole of our lives with the same fullness of commitment and concentration. Only under the shadow of death does life acquire sharpness of relief and intensity of value.

What good is death? It is good because it is a new beginning, our entry into the new world of the age to come. It is not an end point but a starting point. It is not closing the book of life but opening it at page one.

2

Jürgen Moltmann
Tübingen, West Germany

The author of almost two dozen books, Jürgen Moltmann holds doctorates (both earned and honorary) from
the University of Göttingen, Duke University, Emory
University, and Moravian Seminary, among others.

After five years in the pastorate in Bremen, Professor
Moltmann served on the theological faculties at Wuppertal, Bonn, and Tübingen, where he has been since
1967.

Among his special interests outside of theology are
both literature and politics.

He is currently at work on books concerning pneuma-
tology, eschatology, and ecology.

Select Bibliography

The Theology of Hope. New York: Harper and Row, 1967.

Religion, Revolution and the Future. New York: Charles Scribner's Sons, 1969.

Theology of Play. New York: Harper and Row, 1972.

The Crucified God. New York: Harper and Row, 1973.

The Experiment Hope. Philadelphia: Fortress, 1975.

The Future of Creation: Collected Essays. Philadelphia: Fortress, 1979.

On Human Dignity: Political Theology and Ethics. Philadelphia: Fortress, 1984.

Theology Today. Philadelphia: Trinity Press International, 1988.

Creating a Just Future. Philadelphia: Trinity Press International, 1989.

What do you consider the church's most perfect creed (or statement of faith), and why do you think so?

Within the ecumenical movement, we believe that the Nicene Creed is the best. "Faith and Order" is now working on a new interpretation of that creed, an interpretation designed to bring the separated churches back into its orbit once again.

Having said that, however, let me point out but a few of the weaknesses of such a creed. It did not (and could not) prevent the separation of the churches. Indeed, it was the occasion of some divisions. Nor did it seem to have any discernible effect upon the Protestant Reformation, which, like some other great religious movements, succeeded quite well without it.

Furthermore, I do believe that we need a new creed. As a Reformed theologian, I do not believe that the Christian faith can be adequately captured by, or expressed by, any one creed for all time. The church needs to remember (and not be afraid of) the fact that to confess our faith is an ongoing process, one that must be carefully related to whatever situation we find ourselves in at the moment. Because that situation is always changing, the precise form of our confession and of our apologetic must change as well.

What things have made you doubt, and how have you handled them?

My experience as a prisoner of war made me doubt my idealistic German education. It made me doubt the human subject. It made me doubt the goodness of the human will. Those doubts helped turn me to God. They helped to make me a Christian. God made me doubt everything upon which I put my trust as a young man. But I have not doubted God.

What books or theologians have had the greatest influence upon you?

The first theological book I ever read, as a prisoner of war in England, was Reinhold Niebuhr's *The Nature and Destiny of Man.* (But I don't know if I really understood it!)

I also have been shaped by my student days at Göttingen University, especially by the way I learned to understand Martin Luther's theology of the cross and its application to our situation then, as those who were ex-prisoners of war, recently released from the prison camps and the hospitals.

Karl Barth, of course, has had a large influence upon me, but primarily by means of the critical distance from him that I have had to establish, and not by imitation. My liberation from the Barthian circle was made possible primarily by [Arnold] Van Ruler, the Dutch Reformed theologian of Utrecht, especially by means of his theology of the apostolate and his theology of the coming kingdom of God.

What aspect of your thought do theologians continue to misunderstand?

Americans seemed to think of my theology of hope too optimistically. Perhaps they get this from Robert

Schuller's widely publicized emphasis on success. I have attempted to counterbalance this misunderstanding with a stronger emphasis on the cross and on the accompanying notion of the crucified God, which people do understand, at least in some situations. I have received letters from Christians in prison in places like South Africa or Korea. I have heard from those who work with street people or poor people in the United States. Their correspondence makes me believe that those who feel the shadows of the cross fall across them in their circumstances of suffering begin to understand what I meant.

In some ways, of course, I do not regret that some people have misunderstood my books. After all, much understanding begins with misunderstanding.

Do you have any regrets?

A book that I wished to write fifteen years ago, one I still wish to write but have not, is a theology of the Holy Spirit. Similarly, I have postponed—but still wish to write—works on angels and on the devil, or radical evil.

In my first three books, those on the theology of hope, on the crucified God, and on the church and the power of the Spirit, I tried to concentrate my theology on one focus: the focus of hope, or the focus of suffering, etc. In so doing, perhaps my focus was too one-sided. For example, I think now that my criticisms of [Wolfhart] Pannenberg in *The Theology of Hope* were a bit one-sided. I might have been able to invite him into the movement of theological hope if I had not distanced him by overstressing his theology of history.

In that light, I am aware that fifteen or twenty years ago, when debates raged between theological factions like the Barthians and the Bultmannians, we wrote too aggressively, too emphatically. We said too many things just to make a point in a debate. When they are read now, outside that debate, our books seem too combative. I now try to write more relaxed. Who knows if I will succeed!

What is the role of the theologian in the church and in the university?

Every Christian is a theologian. That is because every Christian who thinks of his faith, or thinks from his faith, is theologizing. There are, of course, trained and untrained theologians. The trained theologians should remember to respect those who are untrained, especially in light of what I have just mentioned—the theologianship of all believers. (This fact parallels the priesthood of all believers, of which all pastors should remind themselves.)

The university theologian, by contrast, should not function directly in the service of the church, but in the service of God and the kingdom of God (which are not the same as the church). The university theologian must function in relationship to the members of the other faculties with whom he comes in contact. In that capacity, the university theologian serves as an advocate of the "not-yet believing." He addresses them and dialogues with them.

But the university theologian must not become a servant of any church, or an advocate of any church's teaching. The university theologian has a special dignity and office, which should not be compromised or violated by a church's leadership, who might turn that university theologian into a mere apologist for sectarian teaching. Rome, I think, is most guilty of this.

You see, the theologians have one charisma; the priests have another charisma; and the lay people have another charisma yet. They should work together to correct each other; but they should not transgress against one another.

What is the unfinished task of theology, and what field of inquiry or method of inquiry seems most promising to pursue now?

The unsolved problem of theology is always the recognition of God. The end of that quest will be the end of time, when we see God face to face and all our theological problems begin to disappear. In that way, God is the first problem and the last problem of theology. At the moment, his existence and his presence make us feel some things as problems that we might not otherwise consider problems at all.

And where can we find God, or by what methods can we come to recognize him? As a Reformed theologian, I would say first that God can be found by reading the Bible, especially in the promissory history of the Old and New Testaments. One should also listen to other theologians in the community of theologians, from Augustine to Luther, to Schleiermacher, to Barth. I advise you also to listen to those around you and to yourself.

But I don't believe in methodologies very strongly. I prefer to leave such questions open. At the end of my theological life, perhaps I will write a book on my methods. Then, I suppose, my prolegomena will become my "epilogomena!"

What are the greatest problems facing those in your own religious tradition?

In the Western tradition, we still have a problem understanding the power of God and the powerlessness of Christ. Our tradition tells us that God is, so to speak, apathetic. That is, we say God cannot suffer; only human beings can suffer. We need to restructure or redefine our beliefs about the power and the powerlessness of God in light of the crucifixion and in the aftermath of Auschwitz and Hiroshima.

Protestants, whether liberal or evangelical, also seem to have concentrated too much on human salvation, overlooking cosmic salvation. As a result, we have left the earth exposed to destruction partly as a result of our theological neglect or oversight. Ecological problems are indicative of some of the sins and unsolved problems of our religious tradition. Theologians should begin to see themselves as members of the community of creation, and they should lead the way in helping to rewrite the laws of the nations accordingly, so that animals (for example) become subjects in their own right, not merely objects or projects. Animals have rights.

What advice do you have for those of other traditions, especially American evangelicals?

I don't know enough about American evangelicals to speak about them with much authority or insight. But I do know this: the advantage of American evangelicals is that they start with the biblical tradition, while many of the liberal Christians and theologians just start with their own religious feelings—which is not good ground upon which to build. If, however, we are speaking of American fundamentalists, then I believe that they do not understand what they read.

What is a human being?

I just finished a semester-long course on theological anthropology, so I am acutely aware that it is difficult to answer this short question in a brief but adequate fashion. The shortest answer, of course, is that human beings are the image of God. But that does not say very much.

To expand upon that, however, we can observe that as male and female we humans are God's mirror. As God's mirror, we are to reflect his beauty, his honor, and his will here on earth. Wherever the image of God appears, there God himself becomes indirectly manifest. This fact makes the role of human beings on earth so very critical: we can reflect God. All too often, though, we conduct ourselves in the opposite manner—we reflect the devils!

These considerations tell us that we are to understand the image of God as something relational or functional, not substantively, not as a substance within the human being.

Describe God.

I can't describe God because I've never seen him. But, I've heard about him, and I've heard him calling me by name. When he appears again, I'll know his voice.

What is the Christian gospel, and what is the most effective way to present or defend it in the modern world?

The Christian gospel says that in Jesus Christ all God's promises are "yes" and "amen." The gospel brings the grace of God and the "yes" of God to us.

Under the law we accuse ourselves and others and have such grave doubts about whether or not we can accept ourselves and others or not. In the face of that fact, however, the gospel is God's own great assurance to us. It expresses, it brings, God's hope for us to us. In its light we can see ourselves and our lives differently.

This gospel is presented best not by any threats of hell, but by an invitation to share the great joy of faith and the new perspective on ourselves and on our lives that faith brings.

What do you see as your greatest achievement, or the one of which you are the proudest?

I'm not sure I want to use the word *proudest*. But I do know what pleases me most, and what gives me the greatest satisfaction. It is not my work.

I am most pleased that I came out of the abyss of war and prison camps as a Christian. I am pleased that even in the face of such things I moved from despair and anxiety to faith. For that, I am supremely grateful. It was not my own achievement. But I was turned around and reborn to a living hope in an age of hopelessness and fear. It was an experience to which I owe my life.

I also am grateful to have found somebody with whom to love, to live, and to grow old. Those moments of unearned joy are for me the best moments in life. At

those times I am astounded at my being, my wife's being,
and those of our children. In such moments, all that I
have done, or tried to do, fades away.

How would you like to be remembered?

As I always say to my doctoral students, I want to be
remembered not as a teacher, but as a friend.

What are the beauties and utilities of your theology, and what are its shortcomings?

A hope that makes you certain gives orientation to
your life. We know how valuable this hope is because
we see all around us the sickness of those who have lost
their orientation. They have forgotten that life has
meaning.

Such a hope, however, can also make you believe so
strongly that something better will come along tomorrow
that you actually miss the advantages of the present day.

On the one hand, what is a good life, and what good is life? On the other hand, what is a good death, and what good is death?

A good life is a life blessed by God, and a life to which
you yourself can say, without reservation, "yes." It is a
life you yourself can affirm. A life of this sort is good for
this purpose: the blessing of other people, whether your
family, your community, or even the community of creation at large.

I am not sure that there can ever be a good death.
Perhaps there can be a good death only if you are so old,
so sick, so tired of life, or so shrunken that you cannot
experience life any more. To such a person, death may
be good; death may come as a redemption. But even
then, the survivors mourn because love always wants
the beloved to be alive. That is a sign that no death is
natural. Mourning is a sigh for that new creation where
death will be no more.

In a different sense, there was only one death that was good, and that was Christ's death for us on the cross.

If you could ask any theologian of any time and place just one question, whom would you ask and what would you ask?

I would ask what they think about God, how they understand God, and what has shaped their understanding. I would ask this not only of one person, but of everybody.

I would ask these questions because we can see how the understanding of God as "Abba, Father" changed the life of Jesus after his baptism, how the vision of the living Christ changed Paul, and how Augustine's life was changed by his own understanding of God. (By the way, I do think of Jesus as a theologian, but as one who knew far more about God the Father than any of us!)

3

Wolfhart Pannenberg
Munich, West Germany

Wolfhart Pannenberg earned both his Dr. Theol. and Dr. Theol. (habil.) at the University of Heidelberg. He has received doctorates from the universities of Manchester, Glasgow, and Dublin as well.

Before becoming professor of systematic theology at the University of Munich in 1967, he held similar posts at both Wuppertal and Mainz. Dr. Pannenberg has also been a visiting professor at the University of Chicago, Harvard University, and Claremont School of Theology.

In addition to pursuing his interests in music, art, philosophy, and ancient history, Dr. Pannenberg is working to complete the final two volumes of his much-anticipated *Systematic Theology*.

Select Bibliography

Jesus—God and Man. Philadelphia: Westminster, 1968/1977.

Revelation as History. (Editor.) New York: Macmillan, 1968.

Theology and the Kingdom of God. Philadelphia: Westminster, 1969.

What Is Man? Contemporary Anthropology in Theological Perspective. Philadelphia: Fortress, 1970.

Basic Questions in Theology. 3 vols. Philadelphia: Westminster, 1970, 1971/1983. (Volume 3 was published by SCM, 1973.)

The Apostles' Creed: In the Light of Today's Questions. Philadelphia: Westminster, 1972.

Theology and the Philosophy of Science. Philadelphia: Westminster, 1976.

Faith and Reality. Philadelphia: Westminster, 1977.

Human Nature, Election, and History. Philadelphia: Westminster, 1977.

Ethics. Philadelphia: Westminster, 1981.

Christian Spirituality. Philadelphia: Westminster, 1983.

The Church. Philadelphia: Westminster, 1983.

Anthropology in Theological Perspective. Philadelphia: Westminster, 1985.

Christianity in a Secularized World. London: SCM, 1989.

$\mathcal{OW}$hat do you consider the church's most perfect creed or confession of faith, and why do you think so?

Obviously, it is the Nicene Creed because it is the only truly ecumenical creed of the church.

In Reformation times, Christians thought that the Apostles' Creed had a higher authority than the Nicene because they believed it was written by the apostles. But, of course, we now know this is not true. The Apostles' Creed came from the congregation at Rome. It has never enjoyed the kind of authority claimed or enjoyed by the Nicene Creed, which is an expression of the common faith of the church, the whole church.

Therefore, there is a unique dimension to the Nicene Creed to which nothing is comparable in any other.

Some people, of course, desire to replace the Nicene Creed with a modern confession or interpretation. But, the problem arises that this modern confession might be *another* faith, and not a continuation of the Nicene faith.

What things have made you doubt, and how have you handled them?

I did not really doubt.

That does not mean, of course, that our affirmation of

45

Christianity should not be open to doubt. I do not share the opinion of those who think that the decision to believe should shelter our affirmations of faith from doubt or investigation. One must look at one's beliefs as closely and impartially as possible. But those things do not cause me any concern because I anticipate that God will take care to protect the truth of the gospel. That is why I am not terribly concerned with doubt or doubts. I realize that our human critical judgments are, at best, provisional.

Some things, of course, we can call into question, even reject. I think here, for example, of the virgin birth or the story of Adam and Eve in paradise. The historicity of those stories I doubt. But doubting them is not the same as doubting the Christian faith. Such things are not essentials. Our negative critical assessments here do not shake my confidence in the truth of the gospel.

This is not to say that my faith is impregnable. If the resurrection were disproven, that would be a major blow to my confidence.

Finally—and this is an important point—we must learn to be as critical of the critics of the faith as we are of the faith itself.

What books and what theologians have had the greatest influence upon you?

From the many Christian thinkers of the past, it would be difficult for me to make a choice, so let me mention to you the most influential theologians of our time. First, in biblical theology, I am most indebted to Gerhard von Rad and to the views he has expressed in such books as his *Old Testament Theology*.

In systematic theology the most influential figure has been Karl Barth, whom I hold in high regard, but whom I do not always follow. That is probably because of my medieval training, which stresses philosophical precision and rigor, things in which Barth himself was weak.

Furthermore, although Barth quoted from many theo-

logians, he was imprecise concerning the history of theology. That is, while Barth was a learned scholar by the
standards of his day, by later standards his views are not
fully reliable. Many modern dissertations, for example,
have exposed Barth's misunderstandings of the historical
record. Nor did Barth pay due attention to the historical
exegesis of the biblical writings.

Having said all that, however, let me say again that
Karl Barth was certainly an overwhelming figure in systematic theology.

What aspect of your thought do theologians continue to misunderstand?

There are many. Let me mention but two.

First, my assertion of the historicity of the resurrection is continuously misunderstood. This involves the
question of what the term *historical* means (and what it
does not). The term *historical* is related to the development of historical criteria for the purpose of assessing
traditions that relate past events. Whatever helps us to
evaluate those traditions should be counted among
those criteria. The affirmations that we can make as a
result of these examinations are what is meant by the
term *historical*.

Or, to put it the other way around, if I make a claim
concerning an event, I know that there will be an examination of my claim on the basis of historical criteria. *I
cannot make a claim that something happened in the
past without implying historicity.* Yet, this fundamental
logical fact has been consistently misunderstood.

I am not saying that this is a matter of proof. Many
things that historians and theologians assert or affirm are
not proven. Historical judgment, in that sense, is often
hypothetical. We may not be finally or fully certain. But,
we can often consider such things as *practical* certainties.

Thus, to make a claim to historicity has nothing necessarily to do with proof. It only expresses the confi-

always needs to be done again and again. But doing so, of course, is often a rather personal affair.

In pursuing such a task, I believe we must raise the level of sophistication of the ongoing discussions in the field of theology, especially concerning the criteria of judgment. In systematic theology, one should be concerned with the history of a problem, as well as its contemporary forms. That is, we must know when, how, and why a problem arose before we can adequately address ourselves to it.

We also should concern ourselves with the more general requirements of coherence and consistency. By doing so, I hope Christian theology will reobtain and pursue its task on the highest level of sophistication, which is our best weapon against the present cultural marginalization of theology. If we do, some day our culture will realize that it was not really respectable to despise Christianity.

But, we must not go with the latest fads. I consider liberation theology and feminism to be predominantly faddish and to be largely without serious intellectual content, though some findings from these fields need to be taken seriously.

What are the greatest problems facing those in your own religious tradition?

Confessionalism. People do not seem to realize that *it is enough to be Christian.* I have no sympathy for any kind of slavish confessionalism, whether Lutheran, Reformed, or Roman Catholic. That is, while to be catholic as a Christian is desirable, to be popish is not. We Christians should feel free both to advocate the best things in our respective traditions and to criticize in them what is bad. In other words, as a Lutheran myself, I am aware that it is more desirable to be Christian than to be Lutheran. Or, to put it differently, Christian theology should be ecumenical by definition.

Nevertheless, the various confessional traditions will

remain and should remain. They are important. But they should aim at a Christian synthesis, or a synthesis that is simply Christian. In this light I find that Roman Catholic theologians like Karl Rahner share my vision and concern. Rahner was not only a Roman Catholic theologian, he was a catholic one as well.

From a more global perspective, I believe we Protestant theologians need also to relate to other religions, not just other churches. This, and not secularism, is the great challenge now facing us.

What advice would you have for those of other traditions, especially American evangelicals?

I was pleased to learn recently that many American evangelicals no longer want to be called fundamentalists. That is good. But, they still need to be reminded that one should not seek to base everything on the decision of faith. One should not be afraid of rational, critical investigation. One should trust in God that, if it is true, God's gospel will stand. He will take care of it. He does not need us to shelter it from scrutiny.

American evangelicals need to maintain the faith —which they do. They have not sold out the central Christian affirmations. They must not.

I am displeased when liberals say that we no longer need to ask questions concerning truth. If that were true I would find another occupation. I am pleased that when it comes to asking questions pertaining to truth that evangelicals *do* ask them. Yet, they are afraid of some kinds of examination and criticism, especially biblical criticism. That is unfortunate.

What is a human being?

They are animals, called to the highest dignity, that of companionship with God. Yet, they are deeply troubled beings because they do not dare to live in the light of God.

Describe God.

God is a field of force without limits of extension or power, pervading all reality, and giving rise again and again to new creatures. This the Bible calls Spirit and is identified by Jesus Christ as fatherly love.

What is the Christian gospel, and what is the most effective way to present it and defend it in the modern world?

The Christian gospel is the announcement of God's presence as causing and encouraging the joy of life.

This is best presented not as repentance or penitence, which too often leads to a pathological morbidity. Such preaching deprives us of joy because it robs the gospel of the visibility of its joy.

Nevertheless, in our day we *need* more repentance and penitence. We also need a new morality. But such things are destroyed by this neurotic emphasis.

What do you see as your greatest achievement, or the one that has given you the most satisfaction?

From the moment of my conversion (on the day of Epiphany) onwards, it has been the experience of living in the light of Christ—this is my greatest satisfaction.

In my professional life, I would be deeply gratified to see others go on with the kind of vision I now have for theology in the light of Christ.

How would you like to be remembered?

As a good Christian, one who had confidence in the truth of God.

On the one hand, what are the beauties and utilities of your theology, and, on the other hand, what are its strengths and weaknesses?

These two things are very much bound up with the rational character of my theology, which both attracts and alienates. That is, it draws some, but it also limits the number of those who will appreciate what I am trying to do.

What is a good life, and what good is life? What is a good death, and what good is death?

The second part of your question I do not yet know, though I anticipate that a good death would be one that occurred in peace with God and in gratitude for what he has given us. The same would hold true of a good life. We must accept every new day with thanksgiving and joy. The least God can expect of us is that we must receive each day with gratitude.

Death is good because in dying we make room for others. Life is good if it is spent in self-giving for others. But you can live in that manner only if you believe that life is something for which one ought to be grateful. You see, life should have its satisfaction in itself, each moment. This satisfaction we find primarily in community, primarily in serving others.

If you could ask any theologian of any time or place just one question, whom would you ask and what would you ask?

Perhaps I would ask just the sort of questions you are asking. Or perhaps I would prefer to ask many theologians many questions, questions which would vary in each case. My questions probably would focus on the universality or particularity of some aspects of the Bible. I also should like very much to ask Paul what he actually saw on the road to Damascus.

4

Bishop Graham Leonard
London, England

In addition to his M.A. from Balliol College, Oxford (Honour School of Natural Science), Graham Leonard, the Bishop of London since 1981, has been granted no fewer than six honorary doctorates from schools both in the United States and the United Kingdom—Simon Greenleaf School of Law, Siena College, Westminster College (Fulton, Missouri), Nashota House, and Episcopal Theological Seminary among them.

His current bishopric is his third, before which he served as a parish priest for eight years, as well as diocesan director of education, general secretary of the National Society for Religious Education, and Archdeacon of Hampstead. He has also served as chairman for both the Church of England's Board for Social Responsibility and its Board of Education.

Besides his ecclesiastical and theological concerns, Bishop Leonard's special interests include music, political biography, and poetry. He is currently at work on the 1991–92 Hensley Henson Lectures for the University of Oxford.

Select Bibliography

God Alive: Priorities in Pastoral Theology. London: Darton, Longman and Todd, 1981.

Firmly I Believe and Truly. London: Mowbray, 1985.

Life in Christ. London: Mowbray, 1986.

The Tyranny of Subjectivism. Fulton, Mo.: Westminster College, 1987.

What do you consider the church's most perfect creed or confession of faith, and why do you think so?

Without hesitation, I would say the Nicene Creed. I say so because it is the most universally accepted of the creeds. Of course, I am aware of the controversy surrounding the filioque clause. That notwithstanding, the Nicene Creed is accepted by the great majority of Christians everywhere. This creed represents a crucial point between the Apostles' Creed, on the one hand, and later, less universal creedal developments, on the other.

Furthermore, the Nicene Creed properly maintains the divinity of Christ, which is of the essence of the gospel. The Nicenes clearly declared that our Lord is God.

What things have made you doubt, and how have you handled them?

I do not think that I have ever seriously doubted the existence of God. Rather, my doubts have circled around what I perceived to be his nature or his character.

You see, I was deeply troubled by a universe that seemed to operate according to the paradigm of "dying to live." Something always seems to have to die for something else to live: both man and animals eating other animals in order to survive, for example. I did not then understand the profound way in which dying to live is the face love wears in a fallen world.

As a trained scientist (a biologist), I learned that I had to come face to face with reality, a reality I could not falsify or alter according to my own private preferences. I learned instead that I had to accept reality if I were to take part in redemption. That truth has helped me to deal with my doubts. It has taught me that the pattern of death and resurrection is true love's method of operation.

What books and theologians have had the greatest influence upon you?

I would start with Saint Paul and Saint John, whose writings are not merely "sourcebooks." These men are very real to me. They are not dead people. They speak to me. When I read them, in other words, I am very conscious of receiving something from *somebody*. I am not simply reading a text.

Of the Fathers, Saint Athanasius interests me most, especially on the incarnation. Saint Irenaeus has had a profound effect on me as well.

From the present, T. S. Eliot's *Four Quartets* has had an enormous influence upon my thinking.

Of course, I cannot fail to mention Eric Mascall and Austin Farrer. Mascall I consider perhaps the greatest of modern Anglican theologians.

Finally, there is F. F. Bruce. He treats Scripture as Scripture; and he's a good scholar to boot!

What aspect of your thought do other theologians continue to misunderstand?

First, they find it very hard to understand that I *start* with reality, as far as I can. What I say expresses a response to reality. I begin with that, and not with what suits me.

Second, they cannot see how someone with my firm beliefs can be sensitive pastorally. They think that theological convictions automatically lead one to impose those convictions on others. They do not understand that given firm beliefs one can be flexible, especially as regards the politics of a situation.

In that light, one of the things the gospel says to me is that God has chosen to save us in a way that keeps us free to choose. There is no heavy-handed resort to manipulation. Nor is there a relinquishing of freedom. Thus, God's definite intention to save, and hence God's "firm conviction," does not lead to compulsion. Nor do my theological beliefs, even though I hold them with conviction. Belief in absolutes is most assuredly not incompatible with pastoral compassion or procedural flexibility.

Conversely, I find it so astonishing that liberals, who claim to see intolerance in others, fail to see it in themselves. They pride themselves on tolerance but are intolerant of those who reject liberalism. I've heard it said, though I can not remember by whom, that if you scratch a liberal, you'll find a fascist lurking beneath the surface.

Do you have any regrets?

Yes, for my sins.

That and the fact that I did not study theology at Cambridge in such a way as to be a *professional* theologian. I took what was called the Cambridge Ordination Course. My earlier studies were designed rather to make me a scientist. I have, of course, tried to make up for it. In this respect, Eric Mascall has been very helpful.

Also, because of my pastoral career, my theological reflection has, of necessity, always had a pragmatic cast to it. I would like to have considered theology in a more academic or measured way. Not that I regret the amount of time I had to spend on practical issues—I do not. But such issues often keep me in the pursuit of what are sometimes secondary *theological* issues. As a result, I suppose I have become an intellectual without becoming an academic.

What is the role of the theologian in the church and in the university?

Within the church, the theologian must articulate the meaning of the revelation in which he is living. I feel this passionately: You cannot explain the revelation to your contemporaries unless you actually are experiencing it and being challenged by it. Living in Christ, living in community, living in prayer, living in communion —this is the life of the theologian.

In that light, most of what passes for theology in the university is not theology at all. It is almost always prolegomena only. Real theologizing is drawing out the substance of the gospel itself, not merely circling around the perimeters of the faith (though such things are necessary).

All too often today's theologian begins with unexamined presuppositions and is not interested in correcting them open-mindedly. Here I am thinking of Rudolf Bultmann, who did not challenge his own presuppositions. He simply dispensed them along with the facts. F. F. Bruce, by contrast, does not do that. He is ready always to listen to the Word.

Another problem we now face is the relationship between one's church commitment and one's theological position. There are many (and here I include not theologians only) who choose to dissent from some of the very essentials of the church's confession of faith and *yet who want to stay within the church.* They are free to believe as they like, of course, but they cannot remain in the church. Where is the integrity in such actions? Where is the honor?

What is the unfinished task of theology, and what field of inquiry, or method of inquiry, seems most promising to pursue now?

As is reflected in Ephesians, the task of theology is to understand, with all the saints, what is the length, breadth, heighth, and depth of the wisdom of God. That task, of course, always remains unfinished.

The most important issue of the moment is the relationship between our doctrine of creation and our doctrine of redemption. As the prologue to Saint John's Gospel indicates, the same God who made the world is also the Savior who redeemed it. But we have yet to draw out the implications of such ideas as perhaps we ought. Among the non-Roman churches, the doctrine of creation has largely been neglected. How should we relate to the created world? What is our responsibility to creation, as expounded for us in Genesis?

John Polkinghorne, of Queen's College, Cambridge, has done much excellent work in these and related areas, especially as regards freedom and predictability.

What are the greatest problems facing those in your own religious tradition?

The greatest problem we face today is the decline (or decay) of ontology and the corresponding rise of functionalism, which leads to a resurgent Pelagianism. Ontology is absolutely indispensable for a proper understanding of grace and of justification. I am on the right track only when I can say that what *really* matters is what I am by the grace of God.

Put another way, we are improperly preoccupied with doing, with praxis. We have forgotten (or failed to understand) what things *are.* This is one more indication that we live in a falsely sentimental age.

What advice do you have for those of other traditions, especially American evangelicals?

First, I would urge them to take the doctrine of creation more seriously. Undoubtedly, one of the greatest gaps between the Anglicans and the American evangelicals is in the realm of the sacramental. You cannot bridge that gap without understanding creation and the human person. I thus would advocate a more Hebraic understanding of human beings, whom evangelicals tend to view as merely (or primarily) souls.

Second, we all must take a greater part in enabling creation to reflect the glory of God, which has been obscured by human sins. Creation, you see, is far more than merely the framework within which I am saved.

Third, do remember that it is a characteristic of creation to grow.

What is a human being?

A human being is a psychosomatic unity, made in the image of God, and capable of loving him in mind, body, and spirit. But, human beings also have the dread capacity to neglect and to reject that love.

Describe God.

Here you cannot avoid Saint John, who says that God is love. (This is not at all the same as saying that love is God.) Saint John's teaching drives us to the Holy Trinity, wherein there is a total self-giving of the Father to the Son, and of the Son to the Father. Their mutual love is so transcending that it too is a person.

Because this is how God is, we realize that love is at the core of existence. This is fundamental.

What is the Christian gospel, and what is the most effective way to present and defend it in the modern world?

The Christian gospel is that God chose to make it possible for us to be forgiven and to be restored into fellowship with him, by doing for us what we could not do for ourselves.

To present the gospel most effectively, Christians must live it. There is no substitute for that. That is what draws people to our Lord. (Of course, I am not speaking of the "social gospel.") We worship God in order to be the kind of people who draw others to our Lord.

We must, of course, take account of the culture in which we live. Thus, there is no one particular way to present the gospel that is suitable for all times and places. We must find out what is right and wrong with the world. To do so, we must have eyes that see God at work. That is, we must develop a habitual awareness of the activities of God and then learn to cooperate with them. This leads us to be far more than mere condemnators. It enables us to pick up what is good in a culture and is of God and to bring it to fulfillment. All too often we simply stand in judgment over the culture. This will never do.

What do you see as your greatest achievement, or the thing that gives you the most satisfaction?

Pastoral work—I just love it. Resolving problems *in Christ* is unquestionably the most satisfying thing I do.

In my years of pastoral ministry I have learned that God is very good. He suddenly lifts up a curtain, and you see what has been going on all the while. You see the great movement of God in people's lives, of which you have been a part but about which you had no idea whatsoever.

Just recently, for example, while I was officiating at a confirmation, I asked a woman how it was she had come to faith and to the Anglican Church. She said I had been the cause. I was surprised to hear it. I told her I was sorry, but that I did not remember ever having met her before. She said that she was a receptionist for a large London firm. Her desk was opposite an elevator. One afternoon, the chairman and others met me for a pastoral visit to the firm. I momentarily left the group in order to walk over to her and to greet her personally. That small gesture, as insignificant as it was to me at the time, was significant to her. She had been a receptionist there for a number of years, and no one had ever paused long enough to greet her and to deal with her as a human being. That I had done so greatly impressed her. As she thought about it, she felt grateful to me (and to the God and church I serve) that I took the time to recognize her as a person. She wanted to find out why a busy bishop would do such a thing, which turned her to God and to the church. That's how it all began.

How would you like to be remembered?

I would like to be remembered, above all, as a pastor, one who helped enable people to live with God in eternity.

What are the beauties and utilities of traditional Anglican theology, on the one hand, and what are its weaknesses and shortcomings, on the other?

Anglican theology has always been able to distinguish what is necessary for salvation and agreeable to Scripture from all else. But, we seem to lack sufficient theological integrity and seriousness, which does not come from sloppiness but from our fear of "quenching the smoking flax." As a result, while we have a great deal of smoking flax, we have no fire!

What is a good life, and what good is life? What is a good death, and what good is death?

A good life is a life lived in communion with God, so that what is of God is actually embodied in us. This good life gives us the chance to love God and to live with him.

A good death is one in which we accept the forgiveness God offers and the great blessing that is now about to be ours. Death is good in that it makes clear to us that we are ultimately accountable.

If you could ask any theologian of any time or place just one question, whom would you ask and what would you ask?

I would ask Saint John to tell me how I can better love God and his sheep.

5

Hendrikus Berkhof
Leyden, The Netherlands

Professor Hendrikus Berkhof earned his Dr. Theol. from the State University of Leyden (The Netherlands). In addition, he has been honored with doctorates from the universities of Budapest, Edinburgh, Aberdeen, and Bern.

He was both a minister in the Netherlands Reformed Church and the principal of its theological seminary. He was for many years the church-elected professor in theology (dogmatics and biblical theology) at the State University of Leyden, as well.

Besides pursuing his enduring interest in history, literature, and world politics, Dr. Berkhof has concentrated his latest research efforts on the recent history of doctrine and on a number of shorter studies in dogmatics.

Select Bibliography

The Doctrine of the Holy Spirit. London: Epworth, 1964.

Christ the Meaning of History. London: SCM, 1966.

Christ and the Powers. Scottdale, Penn.: Herald, 1977.

The Christian Faith: An Introduction to the Study of the Faith. Grand Rapids: Eerdmans, 1979/1986.

Introduction to the Study of Dogmatics. Grand Rapids: Eerdmans, 1985.

Two Hundred Years of Theology. Grand Rapids: Eerdmans, 1989.

What do you consider the church's most perfect creed (or confession of faith), and why do you think so?

I have seen Reformed confessions from all over the world, and there are some very good ones. One of the best I know is the Heidelberg Catechism, which is so beautifully and appropriately personal. It begins by asking the catechumen "What is your only comfort in life and in death?"

I must say, however, that I am not fond of creeds or confessions that claim to speak for the entire church at any one time, much less those that claim to speak for the entire church at all times. I prefer those statements that arise from (and address) special situations of tribulation and confession, such as the theses of Barmen.

What things have made you doubt and how have you handled them?

Theologically speaking, I cannot handle my doubts. That is the work of the Holy Spirit.

But what you are asking, of course, is what do I do when I find myself in a situation of doubt. In such circumstances I have discovered that my best medicine is preaching, which I do nearly every week. Preaching compels me to study Scripture, and to do it in the light of all the temptations of my time, and in the face of the secularization of the modern Western world to which I belong and which I try to counteract in various shorter publications.

So, I turn to preaching, to helping others see beyond *their* doubts to Scripture, where they discover their doubts all were anticipated. That has helped me personally. It has always helped, even until now.

What books and theologians have had the greatest influence upon you?

That is difficult to say.

When I was a young student, I was influenced primarily by the Dutch theologians (like Abraham Kuyper) and by those who are known as the mediating theologians, who were trying to combine the most pressing questions of truth and ethics of those times with the Scripture.

Later on, it was Karl Barth, who is by far the greatest of modern theologians.

In some respects, I prefer John Calvin, whom I love very much—much more than Luther, who is too passionate and sometimes confused. As a man of theological discipline, I need clear formulation, and Calvin with his education in jurisprudence and classical culture (humanism) surpasses Luther widely in systematic exactness.

I am also often aided by a layman like C. S. Lewis, whom I myself am returning to frequently in my later years.

In addition, I have spent much time reading the moderns, who have tried to deal carefully and thoroughly with contemporary issues, which is always risky business. It has helped me to see that on some issues the liberals are right and that on other issues the conservatives are right. This study has helped me to feel a kinship both to the open-minded evangelicals, on the one hand, and to the sincerely seeking liberals, on the other.

These are the theologians I like most. Martin Kähler is for me a good example of the first group, Schleiermacher of the second.

But the fundamentalists, I can do nothing with them.

What aspect of your thought do theologians continue to misunderstand?

Some people say to me, "Hendrikus, you are a remarkable fellow. In every book you develop some new heresy!"

Although I sometimes find myself getting angry with those who seem to misunderstand me willingly, I must say that I am not at all a man of polemics. I call to mind the words of Tennyson:

> Our little systems have their day;
> They have their day and cease to be;
> They are but broken lights of thee,
> And thou, O Lord, art more than they.

Those words make me tolerant of the views and criticisms of others. They make me reconsider my beliefs and, if they need revision, to revise them whenever I can. And I have done so repeatedly in my own systematic theology, *The Christian Faith,* which, if it has not actually given rise to misunderstanding, has given rise to disagreement.

In that light, much disagreement centers around my Christology. Theologians like Moltmann and Schillebeeckx seem to want to make me choose between a functional Christology and an ontological one. But I reject those categories. I begin with the humanity of Christ and with his being the true covenant partner with God. I emphasize the uniqueness of this carpenter's Son, who was conceived by the Spirit; who was anointed by the Spirit; and who was as much the servant of the Spirit as vice versa.

Objections also surface over my view of the sacraments and of original sin, as well as over my "universal-istic" conviction that God ultimately will be all in all. You see, I am convinced that there will be no finally successful attempt to plunder anything from God's vineyard. Satan may win many battles, but he will not win the war.

Do you have any regrets?

No, I have no regrets. I have, instead, a feeling of almost miraculous guidance. Even when I was wrong, I have discovered that it was necessary, for God has used it all for the good. And how can I regret what God has used?

Many times I have hoped and prayed that God would use me. When I look at my life, I see that he often has done so. God has used me, and in that light all regrets fall away.

What is the role of the theologian in the church and in the university?

The theologian has to be in the vanguard of the church. That means that the theologian is ahead of the rear guard, but in solidarity with it. But, solidarity does not always mean agreement.

The theologian must look forward. He must have the courage necessary to tackle the difficult questions that perhaps have been avoided by others. In light of the Bible's pluralism, he must speak up in such a way as to *enrich* the church rather than to impoverish its confession.

In the university, the theologian's task is to build bridges and to establish beachheads, so to speak. But, that is not all he does. The time sometimes comes when he is confronted by what is truly wrong. Then he must be angry and polemical. Then he must strive (according to the happy expression of a Dutch theologian) to take away from the error its truth so that he takes away from the error its power.

You see, at the moment there is heavy strife in the theological faculties of some European universities. On the one hand, some believe theology ought to be a descriptive discipline only. These are the proponents of what I call Enlightenment theology. They practice restraint in questions of Christian truth and satisfy themselves with describing the beliefs of others.

But some students find this inadequate. They press the professor with questions like, "What do *you* believe?" That is why other university theologians (me among them) practice what I call classical theology, which adds a personal view to description and replaces restraint with involvement. To do less seems to me to be a failure of nerve.

What is the unfinished task of theology, and what field of inquiry or method of inquiry seems most promising to pursue now?

Through my experience as a doctoral student in theology at Berlin in 1937 I learned to appreciate Karl Barth very much. He was undoubtedly the greatest theologian of our age. That is why modern theology must begin with Karl Barth. But it cannot stop there. Barth, for example, did not adequately relate his theological system to other academic disciplines. He was very hesitant to speak about God's footprints in personal experience and in world history. In response to that second hesitancy, I wrote *Christ the Meaning of History*.

But, we theologians must do more than fill in the gaps in Barth. We also should correct the errors of Barth. He was Christocentric in such a way as to be inadequately pneumatocentric. That is why I wrote my book on the Holy Spirit.

What are the greatest problems facing those in your own religious tradition?

I would say that in the Reformed tradition it is that doctrine which started with Augustine and Calvin, the doctrine called "double predestination." What some good people have tried to do to soften it has all been in vain. We seem to stop at Romans 9 when we ought to go on through Romans 11. Even Calvin once called double predestination that "horrible decree." But what frightened Calvin has not properly frightened us.

What advice do you have for those of other traditions, especially American evangelicals?

My advice is to grow to the full stature of Christ. If they do, their respect for the authority of the Bible will easily lead them to ever new discoveries, by which they may overtake more traditional groups.

I agree with the evangelicals where they say "yes," but not where they say "no," or where they draw various fundamentalisms along with them. Whenever they do so, they will make no spiritual discoveries. They make only fantastic eschatological speculations and charts.

What is a human being?

A human being is the only being in the universe that we know of that was created in the image of God.

Describe God.

You need two words to describe God: "might" (or power) and "love." God is the one whose power is fully used for his love. That is, in God's loving power is our liberty. Or, to follow Karl Barth, God is the loving in the liberty.

To put it differently, God's love and power make it certain that though he loses individual battles, *he will win the war.*

What is the Christian gospel, and what is the best way to present or defend it in the modern world?

The gospel is so rich and has so many sides to it that there is no unambiguous answer to that question, both as to the gospel's precise content and to its presentation.

Good theologians need to know the gospel well enough that they can point to and emphasize the right aspect of the gospel, in the right way, to their own time and place, as Luther did when he pointed out to millions of medieval people the principle of justification by faith and how to get a gracious God. Karl Barth did the same for his age when he denounced Hitler as an idol and rejected "natural theology."

My own experience has been the same. Once Hitler was disposed of, I knew that I had to stop preaching from the Apocalypse and begin preaching out of Haggai and Zechariah about the building of the temple in the name of God. When the escalation of nuclear armaments started, I also had to begin preaching from the Sermon on the Mount concerning Christ and his commandments.

In other words, the gospel is a plurality, the richness and present application of which is revealed in fruitful dialogue. We Christian theologians must relate the gospel to the world in the best possible way in order to keep the gospel from becoming marginalized. We must, of course, stick to the solid doctrine, but we must do so flexibly, under the guidance of the Holy Spirit, whom Jesus promised would guide us. Thus, we have a tension: while we preserve the gospel faithfully, we must present it to the world fruitfully.

What do you see as your greatest achievement, or that which gives you the most satisfaction?

I enjoy writing and teaching, and I'm so glad that God gave me the time and freedom necessary to write my book *The Christian Faith*. I always felt that if I died after that, I could honestly say to God, "That is enough. Thank you so much." But I got more!

Now that I am retired, I no longer work on my own initiative. Rather, I let God lead. As a result, I am overwhelmed with work, especially dealing with or guiding younger theologians in what they write or think.

But to the fact that God has used me and guided me, I can only respond in humble astonishment.

How would you like to be remembered?

If I am to be remembered, I would like to be remembered first as a bridge builder and second as a polemicist, but only in the service of bridge building.

What are the beauties and utilities of your theology, on the one hand, and what are its weaknesses and shortcomings on the other?

The strength of my theology is that it takes account of the many-colored truth of God, and sees its underlying unity. In that way it can tie together things that have not previously been joined, and it can lead to a community and a sharing that otherwise might not happen.

If my theology survives, it may be because I hate absolutisms and am aware of the many-colored wisdom of the gospel. I point anew to the poem of Tennyson that I mentioned earlier. Unlike some fundamentalisms, which impose far too much on people, my theology is less likely to collapse under its own weight.

But, my beliefs are subject to various theological temptations. By being a bridge builder and by tying together things that have been unconnected, I have perhaps not been keen enough to the dangers of theological error. Because of my ecumenical inclinations, I can too easily fall into heresy.

What is a good life, and what good is life? What is a good death, and what good is death?

The answer to your first question is found in the Great Commandment: love the Lord your God with all your mind and with all your heart, and your neighbor as yourself. A good life, then, is when you love all three: God, yourself, and your neighbor.

Death serves the purpose of helping to renew us by being the dark tunnel through which we need to pass.

That is, death shows us the preliminariness of this world and of this life. Death is an interim state, serving God's purpose of exorcism and purgation.

A good death is when we can leave this life in gratitude.

If you could ask any theologian of any time or place just one question, whom would you ask and what would you ask?

Here you ask a playful question, but one that has meaning.

Here you also ask far more than I can answer. Perhaps I can only echo what Karl Barth once said: "When I come to heaven, I would like to ask Schleiermacher about the Holy Spirit and Bonhoeffer about what exactly it was that he disapproved of in my books and why."

(Karl Barth was a great admirer of Bonhoeffer, and Bonhoeffer's disapproval pained him very much.)

6

Dorothee Sölle
Hamburg, West Germany

Dorothee Sölle earned her Dr. Phil. from the University of Göttingen and her Dr. Theol. (habil.) from the University of Cologne.

She has lectured at the universities of Cologne, Mainz, and Hamburg. She also has been appointed many times a visiting professor at Union Theological Seminary in New York.

Her interest in music complements her many current projects, most notable among them being her involvement in the conciliar process of the World Council of Churches (WCC) and its various concerns for justice, peace, and ecology.

SELECT BIBLIOGRAPHY

Christ the Representative: An Essay in Theology after the "Death of God." London: SCM, 1967.

Political Theology. Philadelphia: Fortress, 1974.

Suffering. Philadelphia: Fortress, 1975.

Death by Bread Alone: Texts and Reflections on Religious Experience. Philadelphia: Fortress, 1978.

Revolutionary Patience. Maryknoll, N. Y.: Orbis, 1979.

The Arms Race Kills Even Without War. Philadelphia: Fortress, 1983.

Of War and Love. Maryknoll, N. Y.: Orbis, 1983.

To Work and to Love: A Theology of Creation. (With Shirley A. Cloyes.) Philadelphia: Fortress, 1984.

The Window of Vulnerability. Philadelphia: Fortress, 1990.

Note: Some American and British publishers occasionally spell Sölle's last name "Soelle."

Ohat do you consider the church's most perfect creed or confession of faith, and why do you think so?

I have trouble with the idea of "most perfect" in this context. That is because in order to stay faithful to Christ in our ever-changing situation the Christian's creed must change as well. And, because faith is our response to a living God, we need to ask what God is saying to us today—which might well be different from what God was telling the church in the time of the apostles or of the Reformation.

Having said that, however, let me go on to affirm the Apostles' Creed, with which I grew up. You see, it is very important to have a creed and to struggle with it. Several years ago I was called upon to rephrase that creed for current theological, liturgical, and political purposes. This was a difficult task, but one well worth-while.

The other historic creed I would mention is the Barmen confession, which is one of the few things inside German Protestantism for which I feel some pride, especially regarding its emphasis on Christ in life and death and Christ above all races, which is very important to me.

What things have made you doubt, and how have you handled them?

Let me answer you in two ways: first, theologically and intellectually, and second, spiritually and existentially.

First, I grew up in a liberal family where the Bible was seen as merely one voice among many others. It was not *the* Word of God to us. Thus, even though some of my grandfathers were pastors, the critical spirit of the post-Enlightenment was strong in my parents' home. As a result, I had many doubts about Christian doctrine and the truth of the biblical narrative. For example, the virgin birth of Jesus then seemed to me untrue. I also doubted if such ideas were good for anything. I decided at that time to find out what was possible for a modern person to believe. You see, I was not really a Christian when I first began my study of theology. Reading Rudolf Bultmann aided me enormously in this regard.

Second, questions like "Why does God not intervene?" or "Why is history so bloody?" or "Why do the evil prosper?" raised doubts in me. I want God to come and convince the leaders of the world to stop doing what they do. They go to Mars and to the moon but they do not solve the problems of even one of the children of this world. So I ask God, "Why are you so small?" Why do you let people deny you?" I ask the apocalyptic question, "How long, O Lord?"

I have not yet answered such questions. Perhaps I never will. But from such questions I have discovered that faith must learn to live with its own shadow. Struggling with these things has helped me to develop a little of the "revolutionary patience" about which I have written.

I shall probably never fully escape my doubts. Furthermore, I shall always mistrust those who have no doubts of their own.

What books and theologians have had the greatest influence upon you?

I would like to start with Paul. Struggling with his thought has been one of the deepest influences on my thinking, especially Paul interpreted by Luther. However, I doubt the idea that there is nothing at all good in the human being. I have a less pessimistic (and perhaps more creative) anthropology. I agree with the Quakers, who focus on the inner light that makes us see what is right and do it. They understand that we are able to practice the faith and not just talk.

For many years I also have lived with the thought of Søren Kierkegaard, who in many ways was the father of my development into Christianity itself. I am thinking here of the immensely important distinction he draws between being an admirer of Christ and being his follower. An admirer simply looks at Christ and says how wonderful or how superior he is when compared to us. But a follower of Christ actually imitates him in the rough and tumble struggles of this world. Christianity is for followers.

From contemporary theology, I have been influenced by Rudolf Bultmann, as I said, and by Dietrich Bonhoeffer, who taught me that discipleship is costly. I am so impressed by Bonhoeffer, who occupied himself with a life of ethics and with writing about ethics, even in the face of death itself.

What aspect of your thought do theologians continue to misunderstand?

Two things, chiefly.

First, they often did not understand my insistence upon the powerful metaphor of the death of God, which arose out of existential doubts concerning the concept of the all-powerful God, who sits in heaven and serenely looks down while people are going to Auschwitz—but who does not stop it, even though, in this theology, he could easily do so. Such a concept, such a contradiction, such a God, had to die. He was replaced by the suffering Savior, by the crucified God, and by the body of Christ (the church).

Second, people criticize me because I am not much interested in the idea of life after death. I am an imminentist. I focus on this world, and I reflect on it. I am interested primarily in history, and not what lies behind or beyond it. This others do not understand because they want so badly to extend themselves into eternity, which is thoroughly narcissistic and excessively individualistic. This is not what Christ had in mind. Perhaps this desire is something we ought to examine with the help of Mr. Freud.

Do you have any regrets?

I have some regrets, especially here in Germany, where I never made it into the theological faculties. I have remained an outsider. They never hired me because the theological faculties here are strictly male and under male control. I was excluded because of the sexual dynamics of the theological establishment and because of my leftist theology and politics. But I am not bitter. I have found my true self by writing and by my occasional teaching assignments, primarily in the United States.

I also regret that liberation theology has not been very strong inside of the First World. I wish it would become more well-established. We simply must overturn the injustice we create for two-thirds of the human family and begin to live out our Christian faith.

What is the role of the theologian in the church and in the university?

We trust in theologians too much. We should diminish the role of the theologian in the church. We must understand more fully the discipleship of all believers and the capacity of all believers to be theologians. To be formally educated is not the most important ingredient in the making of a theologian.

For example, in liberation theology we say that the poor are the teachers of theology. By listening to the poor, by examining their plight and trying to alleviate it, we understand the gospel better than we would by listening to a Harvard professor. I learned a great deal about such things by reading Ernesto Cardenal, who, though he is a learned theologian, employs his skills as a supporter of local communal faith and practice and not as its leader. I like the hermeneutics of that. It brings the theologian down to earth and makes the theologian more productive.

In the university, however, we need *more* theologians, not fewer. For example, science needs a conscience. It needs self-control. Even the scientists themselves admit as much. Thus, the theologian has a new importance in the academic community. Theologians must protect creation from science and technology, which have become gods, so to speak, and led us into the present ecological crisis. Theologians must stand up for the poor, the voiceless—the fish, the birds, the animals.

But, let me say now that I am alarmed by the way in which many current theologians have adjusted themselves into the university. Many academic thinkers have permitted the scientific community to set the agendas and establish the methods for the modern dialogue between theologians and the other academics. I prefer the older method of theologians like Barth and Bultmann, who were not merely academics, but who were concerned with how to preach and to proclaim the gospel, not merely to accommodate on someone else's terms. They refused to segregate themselves from the concerns of ordinary people. They did not lock themselves away in an ivory tower of sterile academic jargon.

You see, even in the university, I want to identify with the oppressed. I want to voice their concerns. *That* is where God acts. As a theologian, I want to act with God.

**What is the unfinished task of theology, and what
field of study, or method of study, seems most
promising to pursue now?**

I think it is liberation, which is another word for salvation. That is, the task now is what it always was—the
salvation, or liberation, of the world.

In our day this means that we must uproot economic
injustice and war. It means the conservation and integrity
of creation. These, specifically, are the major portions of
the unfinished task of theology.

To do so, one must study the context and the details of
the oppression now facing us. We must employ the best
methods of amelioration at our disposal. We must study
today's grim situation very carefully. We Christians then
must introduce a new perspective into the modern dis-
cussion, and that is the perspective of the victim. We
must learn to see the world from the point of view of the
oppressed. We must ask "Who suffers?" "What does it
mean to be weak or poor?" This helps us to come closer
to the view of Christ.

We must never delude ourselves into thinking that
what is required of us is some allegedly neutral or super-
ficially scientific study. We must be partisans!

**What are the greatest problems facing those in your
own religious tradition?**

Obedience.

Obedience has become a misunderstood and cor-
rupted concept. We seem to obey only the state or only
the powerful. We lack a resolve, or intention, to resist
evil. I see Christ as a resister, one who did not take the
sword and one who did not take money. But we German
Protestants seem to be far too loyal to the state. This has
led us into the greatest catastrophe of our century:
Nazism. The guilt of most Christians in Germany in this
regard is not that they perpetrated these horrible crimes,
but that they stood by silently, simply watching.

Perhaps this stems from Luther himself, who was so intent upon freeing himself from the Roman Catholic Church, but who was so obsessed with the necessity of a powerful state. An unfortunate line can be drawn from Luther to Hitler. I hope we have now taken at least a few steps away from it.

What advice do you have for those of other traditions, especially American evangelicals?

I would urge them to read the Bible from the perspective of the poor, and to see and feel God's cry for justice.

You can say that God is good and loving and merciful, but if you do not see that this means economic justice, then you miss seeing God and you see only an idol.

It may be painful for American conservatives to do so, but they must see themselves through the eyes of the poor. Not that they are to be disloyal to their country, but that they also are to be loyal to the *other* America, the poor America, as well.

Robert McAfee Brown has done this very well. He reads the Bible from the "underside" of history.

What is a human being?

A human being is a creative, living body and soul, made in the image of God.

We distort this. We think humans are in the image of a machine. We should stick with the old idea of *imago Dei.*

That is, when we ask ourselves what God is like, we must answer by looking at what God does. It is then we realize that we who are in God's image can act in that same way: lovingly. As the rabbis taught long ago, just as God gave clothes to Adam and Eve, we should clothe the naked. Just as God fed Elijah with the help of a raven, we should feed the hungry. We must, and we can, be imitators of God because we must, and we can, do what God did for us: namely, to love our neighbor.

Describe God.

God is the power of life, creativity, energy, and change *in relation.*

But this power is not to be seen as something that only God has. Nor is it something that God desires to reserve for himself alone. God's power is good, and good power wants to be shared. It wants to empower others. God wants to empower us to do the works of love. In this regard, therefore, God does not order us or command us so much as he invites us to share in his power. That is why we need a new set of metaphors for God as the living and loving empowerer.

What is the Christian gospel, and what is the most effective way to present it and defend it in the modern world?

It surely is to love God above all things and your neighbor as yourself.

This is presented best in our deeds, not in our thoughts or feelings. We are our brother's keeper. God asks us what he asked Cain. We must avoid Cain's response, and *be* the keeper of our brothers. And by that I mean all endangered living beings, human and otherwise.

Some say this asks too much of us. We are made to hate, they say. We are made to exploit, to compete, not to love. Perhaps they are right. Such goodness is rarely attained. (As Gandhi said, Christianity would be a good idea, if it were tried.) But, I believe we *are* made to love. To believe this, however, I need Kierkegaard's leap of faith, for my rational side tells me the opposite. It tells me we are terribly aggressive monsters.

What do you see as your greatest achievement, or the thing that gives you the most satisfaction?

I am most satisfied with the development of theological thought and language, at least as far as I have tried to develop it for the purpose of liberation.

For thirty years I have tried this, and the style and perspective of Christian theology seems to have changed. I think that in this I have helped. I now feel less alone and less isolated in the theological discourse. This has helped me to understand and to feel more at home within the concept of "the people of God." In effect, it seems as if, over the last several years, the church has come home to me, especially as regards the movements of peace, justice, and the integrity of creation. I am, for example, especially grateful for the special spirit of *Kirchentag* that we enjoy here in West Germany.

How would you like to be remembered?

I would like to be remembered as a teacher of liberation theology, as a writer of poems and prayers, and surely as a mother and grandmother.

What are the beauties and utilities of liberation theology, and what are its weaknesses and shortcomings?

It is an aid to those who work, who struggle, and who strive. It empowers them. It also comforts or consoles them in the hour of defeat. I get letters from many who have passed through such dark hours and who say that they were helped by my thoughts.

On the other hand, some tell me that my theology is only for the strong—not the weak, not the disturbed, not the aged, not the dying. They tell me it is a theology for those who can *do,* but not for those who cannot. It does not address the downtrodden and the marginalized. It is *about* them; but it is not *for* them.

They also say I ask too much, that only the strong can do what I ask. It hurts me to hear this, because I think they do not realize that God will empower us if we listen and obey. They have forgotten that we *all* are beggars.

But, we inherit the Son, and with him the power of love. It is Bonhoeffer's costly discipleship.

What is a good life, and what good is life? What is a good death, and what good is death?

First, a good life is empowered to work and to love. That does not necessarily mean happiness. Work and love can be combined with loss, defeat, and destruction. But work and love do define our place in the world. They help us grow. And that is the good of life, not merely the good life.

By the way, we need to cling to the idea of the goodness of life. Without it we would never learn to work or to love. We should agree with God that existence is very good.

Second, as Saint Francis says, death is our sister, not merely our enemy. It must be faced the way my eighty-six-year-old mother now faces it: truthfully, and without denial, illusion, or bitterness. That is, we must see death the same way we see birth, which is both painful and natural. We must accept it. We must learn to die satisfied with life.

The good of death is that it is actually the renewal of life. We all have our appointed and limited time on earth. When the time of death comes, we should say to God, "Thank you for this life," and then gratefully and obediently give it back. You see, death is created by God, and not, as some say, by the devil. And what God has made is good.

But this does not mean that the death we create by hunger or by war is good. It is not.

If you could ask any theologian, past or present, just one question, whom would you ask and what would you ask?

I would like to ask Karl Barth why he was so sexist. It seems so self-contradictory. He is so good otherwise. He was able to capture so much mutuality and equality. But then he falls back.

I would also like to ask Søren Kierkegaard why he did not marry Regina. Would that not have been theologically proper? Why did he not believe in God's transforming incarnated love?

7

Gareth Moore, O. P.
Oxford, England

Gareth Moore, O.P., earned his B.A. in politics, philosophy, and economics, his B.Litt. in philosophy, and his B.A. and M.A. in theology, all from Oxford University.

After teaching mathematics and Bible in Zambia for two years, he eventually assumed his present post as an instructor of the English Dominicans at Blackfriars, Oxford.

Besides pursuing his love of music, Father Moore is currently at work on a book about Christian sexual ethics.

Select Bibliography

Believing in God: A Philosophical Essay. Edinburgh: T. and T. Clark, 1988.

*W*hat do you consider the church's most perfect creed or confession of faith, and why do you think so?

I prefer the Nicene Creed. I do so, first, because it is traditional. This is very important. It provides us with a link to the past. As such, it reminds us that the church's theology is not simply a product of the current generation. Theology, in other words, does not belong only to us.

Second, the Nicene Creed helps us to resist the temptation to be too exact. Within bounds, it frees us from the pressures of excessive precision, and it allows us a degree of latitude and creativity.

What things have made you doubt, and how have you handled them?

I think I can honestly say that I have never doubted the existence of God, at least not since I came to believe. But, I have often wondered about what exactly it is we mean when we say things like "Jesus is divine," or how one should understand the church, especially its claims regarding teaching authority. Such questions are not so much doubts as they are inquisitive musings and (as yet) incomplete attempts at understanding.

What books and theologians have had the greatest influence upon you?

After Scripture itself, it has been [Ludwig] Wittgenstein's *Philosophical Investigations,* which brought me a sensitivity to the variety of ways we work with words. It encouraged in me a more sensitive approach to the Bible, for example, rather than my previous more narrowly logical approach. By that I have been enriched, and for that I am grateful.

Do you have any regrets?

Yes. I sometimes tend not to be overly careful when I write. That is, I do not always stop to point out all the little caveats that perhaps I should. I often let the reader supply them. This is risky.

What is the role of the theologian in the church and in the university?

Because the words of those in ecclesiastical authority are important, and because authority is dangerous and can be misused—especially by means of words—the function of the theologian in the church is at least a partly critical one. The theologian should learn to be properly critical of authority. The spirit of criticism is one of the fundamental Christian liberties.

Within the university, academic theologians should try to present the gospel for our own times, a skill they can learn only if they study the past. We are to reformulate and re-present the gospel because the audience is always changing.

I believe it is important both for Christianity and for theology that we keep alive an academic presence, and that we keep alive the skills by which we can understand our faith. By this I mean even simple things like Greek or history. Within academic theology it is also very important that we keep alive the religious dimensions of theology, which is not a merely academic endeavor. We also need to keep alive the very important fact that Christianity is intellectually tenable. Serious, intelligent people can be Christians. In the university, this can be forgotten.

In both cases, however, whether the critical or the evangelistic, the theological enterprise is anti-fundamentalistic.

What is the unfinished task of theology, and what field of inquiry, or method of inquiry, seems best to pursue now?

The theological task is an ongoing task. It's always been unfinished and never will be finished, at least not in this world. It is a task that needs to be repeated in every generation, perhaps repeatedly within every generation.

To do so effectively, the theologian needs to initiate a full-scale engagement with modern academic disciplines. The theologian must be widely knowledgeable, and must not willfully neglect the "ologies"—anthropology, sociology, etc. (I am not saying, of course, that these disciplines are a *substitute* for theology.) For example, in our sexual ethics and in our theology of marriage, we theologians often show that we are ignorant of reality and of modern science and its methods. This ignorance frequently results in untrue sweeping generalizations.

What are the greatest problems facing those in your own religious tradition?

I can't see that the problems facing Catholics are noticeably different from the problems any Christian faces. That is, they are the problems of Christianity in general, and they are not peculiar to any one tradition. We all face the problems of how to live, of what to do, and of what to think, even on issues as wide in scope and large in scale as national and international politics.

What advice do you have for those of other traditions, especially American evangelicals?

I'd invite them to have a look at the Catholic tradition. If they do, they are going to find a church with both a deep conviction and a deep tolerance. They will learn that though the ship is sailing through rough waters, it will stay afloat, thanks to God.

They also will discover that we maintain an appreciation of the arts, which can be lost in Protestantism. Art is one of the greatest glories of what is human, and what is human has a place in the church. The Catholic Church has learned to make room for a proper humanism.

What is a human being?

A human being is a linguistic animal. By "linguistic" I mean that talk is a lot of what we do, and it reflects a lot of what we are. We are "animals" in that we have bodies. We are not merely spiritual creatures somehow trapped in flesh.

Christianity makes room for the body and the senses. Christianity takes into account our *entire* being. That is part of what gives rise to the sacraments and to the arts in the church.

Describe God.

While there are many descriptions of God, there is no privileged description of God, unless one speaks of the scriptural images. When we do, we realize that God is like Jesus Christ. Thus, if you ask *what* is God like, the answer is that he is not like anything. But, if you ask *who* is God like, the answer is he is like Jesus.

To understand God, therefore, you must read the Gospels.

What is the Christian gospel, and what is the best way to present it or defend it in the modern world?

It is this: if you want to understand how to live, and if you want to understand what the world is all about, then you must learn to love as Christ loved.

How you convey this to others depends upon the people around you. The worst possible way is to stand on a street corner, with a Bible under your arm, shouting into empty air. Such people believe that God has called them to preach. But somehow they've neglected the task of getting people to *hear*. Everything depends upon how people hear. You must discover how they do it and then adapt yourself to it.

Though perhaps too many Christians now speak in such terms, I am convinced that people should sometimes be shown the awful possibility of final damnation and of being completely lost. It must be taken seriously.

What do you see as your greatest achievement, or the one that gives you the most satisfaction?

I don't really think of things in those terms. That is, I don't often get proud. I get excited. I get excited by thinking about sex, by music, by sunny days.

You see, I'm not really an *achiever*. I just get grabbed by things. God grabs me. God is attractive. God has to do with the attractiveness of life and with the richness of existence. To me, that is exciting, and that is an important aspect of my faith.

How would you like to be remembered?

I'd like to be remembered as someone who had written something of value. But what it might be, I don't know.

Oh yes, and for not being too awful a person!

What are the beauties and utilities of Roman Catholic theology, and what are its weaknesses and shortcomings?

The answer to both sides of your question is "tradition."

Like most good things, Catholic tradition is a two-edged sword. Positively, our tradition tells us that theology is an enterprise of reason and is, therefore, a human enterprise, one that challenges all our faculties. Negatively, our tradition is sometimes that by which the past imprisons us and holds us captive.

What is a good life, and what good is life? What is a good death, and what good is death?

A good life is a life lived in accordance with the gospel. That is, it is a life of love, a life lived in imitation of Christ. A good life is also a happy life, insofar as a happy life is possible. Others, of course, can make you miserable, and, to a degree, that is not up to you. But, if you are making yourself miserable, then you are not living a good life.

But what good is life? That is perhaps not possible to answer, simply because life is its own good end. It does not need an external justification to make it good. It is not good *for* anything outside itself, unless you want to say that somehow our lives can be good for God.

I don't see how death is very much good either. I confess I have not *thought* much about death—though I have *worried* about it a great deal. I can imagine, however, that a good death is one died in pursuance of the gospel. A good death is also a death that comes not as a frustration of what you hold dear in life, but as its fulfillment. You see, if you live to amass things, then your death will be a frustration of your life because you can't take things with you. But if you live a life of love for God and your fellow man, then your death will be your life's fulfillment.

Yet, given my poor spiritual state, all this sounds too lofty. After all, this is my fear: It's too early to die; there are still many things I want to do.

One of the beneficial functions of death is that it forces us to take life seriously. By it, we understand that this life matters a great deal. Death helps us to appreciate that fact. Because death's approach is uncertain, it forces us to get our life right—*right now.*

If you could ask any theologian of any time or place just one question, whom would you ask and what would you ask?

I couldn't begin to answer that question; first, because my reading is so poor, and second, because theology and theologians are so rich that there is no one "key question" to ask of any one particular thinker. There are, of course, theologians with whom I'd like to go for an afternoon stroll. But I have no specific question.

8

Sister Benedicta Ward
Oxford, England

The author of a number of highly regarded works on the history of Christian piety and theology, Sister Benedicta Ward was, until recently, associated with the Centre for Medieval and Renaissance Studies, in Oxford.

She received her B.A. from Manchester University and her D. Phil. from Oxford University.

Her abiding interest in medieval history finds its latest manifestation in her current research project, which is a volume on the cult of relics in the Middle Ages.

Select Bibliography

Anselm of Canterbury: A Monastic Scholar. Oxford: SLG, 1977.

Prayers and Meditations of Saint Anselm. New York: Penguin, 1979.

Julian Reconsidered. Oxford: SLG, 1980.

Sayings of the Desert Fathers. Oxford: Mowbray, 1980.

Lives of the Desert Fathers. Oxford: Mowbray, 1985.

The Wisdom of the Desert Fathers. Oxford: SLG, 1986.

Harlots of the Desert: A Study of Repentance in Early Monastic Sources. Kalamazoo, Mich.: Cistercian, 1987.

Miracles and the Medieval Mind: Theory, Record, and Event. Philadelphia: University of Pennsylvania Press, 1987.

*W*hat do you consider the church's most perfect creed or confession of faith, and why do you think so?

I would say it is the confession of faith of the eunuch of Candace in Acts 8:37: "I believe that Jesus Christ is the Son of God." I say this because that confession contains the very center of the Christian faith, and all that is necessary.

Among the more formal creeds, the best is the Apostles' Creed, because it is simple and memorable. A creed need not be much more than that. A creed, after all, is simply a peg on which to hang things.

What things have made you doubt, and how have you handled them?

It may perhaps sound extremely arrogant, but I have never ever doubted the existence of God.

I have never doubted redemption; but I have doubted whether or not *I* was redeemed. I have never doubted love; but I have doubted whether or not *I* was loved.

I have doubted myself, however, and my ability to deal effectively with the universe.

What books and theologians have had the greatest influence upon you?

The Bible, especially Saint John's Gospel and the Psalms. Their effect on me is not so much by my choice, but from hearing them over and over in the church and in the daily offices. They are, so to speak, part of the air I breathe and the water in which I swim.

Outside the Bible, I would mention the hymns of Charles Wesley.

In addition to them, I would be quick to add the prayers and meditations of Saint Anselm, which I translated, and which I lived with for nine years, giving them my closest possible attention. I also have been guided by the Venerable Bede and his ecclesiastical history, his commentaries, and his sermons. Both Anselm and Bede have proved themselves soul friends to me, and their wisdom works within me and upon me.

What aspect of your thought do theologians continue to misunderstand?

One very irritating misconception is that they think that because I am a nun I must be religious, pious, and therefore uncritical. They seem not at all to understand that I am unsympathetic to mysticism. I dislike the zany, the emotional, the out of the way, the weird. I don't like being put in that class.

Furthermore, they misunderstand asceticism. They view it as if it were an imposition. But it is chosen! They view it as if it were a denial of life. But it is a choice of life! They think, too, that we nuns are enormously good and enormously influential with God. "Pray for us," they say. But who prays for the nuns? We are in need of mercy, too. We are not the professionally good.

Do you have any regrets?

I'm sorry if what I've written is not somehow transparent of Christ. But I say "I'm sorry," not "I regret." Regretting, I believe, is a problem. But sorrow gives new life. Of one thing I am convinced: "Tis grace has brought me safe thus far, and grace will lead me home."

What is the role of the theologian in the church and in the university?

I would have thought that the theologian's job is to push forward the boundaries of thinking about God.

I would like to think that the theologian is the one who prays correctly, not the one who merely thinks correctly. Christianity, after all, is not only a way of thinking. We must ask ourselves "Who is the theologian?" But, in order to answer that question properly, we must know the difference between knowing about and knowing.

Now, concerning the role of the theologian in the university, I must say that Bishop Kallistos Ware does this very magnificently in Oxford. Nevertheless, there is a danger in teaching theology in the university because theology can then become a subject like all other subjects: liable to destruction by fallen minds. That, surely, is of limited value. Whether in the church or the university, theologians are not there to put one another down. Yet this they often do. As a result, they sometimes destroy the root of faith of their weaker fellow believers, and even of one another.

It is also important that there be a center of prayer within the university. Even one person in an institution, standing in repentance before God, can be a priest for the healing of the whole.

What is the unfinished task of theology, and what field of inquiry, or method of inquiry, seems most promising to pursue now?

Understanding the Scriptures according to the Spirit is vital.

For more than fifty years, the study of the Scriptures has been philological and historical. That's finished. We've done enough.

But there has been nearly two thousand years of inter-
preting the Scriptures with the heart, which now seems
to have gone out of fashion. There's still a rich vein to be
mined here. We need to find out what God is saying to
us *personally,* on every page.

We ought to go about it first historically, of course.
One can, and should, apply one's mind to a verse both
critically and acutely. But Christ is Lord of the heart as
well as the mind. As Saint Bonaventure has indicated,
there is a spiritual hermeneutic, not simply a grammati-
cal/historical one. Both are required. But the former
assumes that the page is, in a sense, *alive.* We believe
that he who seeks the living God in Scripture will not be
disappointed.

What are the greatest problems facing those in your own religious tradition?

I believe our biggest threat is secularism, or the sense
that we somehow should adjust our gospel and ourselves to the rules of the world and all that goes with it,
such as its lack of confidence in the grace of God or its
loss of meaning, which cuts us all off from our roots.
This despising the past is a large part of secularization,
and we Christians should resist it. After all, we received
the gospel itself from the hands of the dead. What would
be our fate if we were to have ignored them?

We must, of course, speak to people in a way they can
understand, but we must not change the truth into a
half-truth in so doing.

What advice do you have for those of other traditions, especially American evangelicals?

Face to face with an American evangelical, one with
whom I was acquainted, I might be able to answer such a
question. But I cannot adequately address the needs of
an entire American religious movement. But to anyone I
would say: "Love and do not be afraid."

What is a human being?

I don't know.

But I think that when I see Christ I shall know, because the fullness of humanity is hidden with Christ in God and is a secret that will be revealed. In other words, insofar as I know Christ, I know humanity, real humanity.

Describe God.

"God," just "God."

There is nothing else to say about God than "God."

God does not have a predicate. In that sense, I cannot describe him.

What is the Christian gospel, and what is the best way to present it or defend it in the modern world?

The gospel, the truly good news, is that God was in Christ reconciling the world to himself.

This is, however, not merely something I *say*. I hope, instead, that it is something that, before I die, God will have made evident through me. I hope, as well, that when I die God will have made it evident to me that his gospel is for me. I stake my life on that expectation.

God knows what he's about. We don't have to worry. But we do have to say with Wesley: "O, God, revive thy church, and begin with me." Those who are thus revived are fountains of water, healing water, water of love, mercy, and humility.

What do you see as your greatest achievement, or what gives you the most satisfaction?

The sort of thing that makes me fall down before God with tears of thanksgiving is when someone lets me know that somehow, or in some way, God has used me for their benefit or blessing.

How would you like to be remembered?

With Thomas Merton's translation of *Laudabilitas vincit:* "She did all right."

What are the beauties and utilities of your theology, and what are its weaknesses and shortcomings?

As an Anglican nun, I find freedom, solitude, silence, and space. It is life to the end. It is all life. It is all the faithfulness of God, and it is an *enormous* gift.

The weakness of it is that it can easily become *my* life, *my* theology, *my* own private possession. I constantly need to break out of that.

What is a good life, and what good is life? What is a good death, and what good is death?

These two really are the same question.

Like Anselm and Bede, we ought to live so as to be able to say that we are not afraid to die.

Before God we have no righteousness. Thus, self-justification is pointless in the face of death. After death comes the judgment. There's simply no point in trying to justify your life. Quite the opposite is true: What makes a life good is that it fall into the hands of God. That alone dispels fear.

When a nun dies, for example, then I myself can see there a completed sacrifice. She has been fully placed into the hands of God, both in life and in death, and that is what makes both her life and death good.

If you could ask any theologian of any time or place just one question, whom would you ask and what would you ask?

I would ask Julian of Norwich, "Do you now know just what is that 'great deed' that shall be done?"

I also would ask Bede, "Did you ever see the Lindesfarne Gospels?" It is the most beautiful book in the world. He saw it, I suppose, but he never mentioned it!

9

Thomas Torrance
Edinburgh, Scotland

The author of more than twenty books and the editor of many more, Thomas Torrance received his M.A., B.D., and D.Litt. from the University of Edinburgh and his D.Theol. from the University of Basel. He is also a fellow of both the British Academy and the Royal Society.

In addition to a decade of parish ministry, Dr. Torrance has served on theological faculties in both America and Scotland. Most recently, he served for twenty-seven years as professor of Christian dogmatics at the University of Edinburgh. He is also former moderator of the General Assembly of the Church of Scotland.

Among his special interests are evangelism, ecumenism, and Jewish/Christian relations. He also maintains a keen interest in mission work among the Chiang tribes of western China.

At present, Dr. Torrance is at work on a lecture for the International Academy of Philosophy of Science and the Centenary of Fribourg University in Switzerland. He is also writing a volume concerning the doctrine of God.

Select Bibliography

Calvin's Doctrine of Man. London: Lutterworth, 1949.

Space, Time and Incarnation. New York: Oxford, 1969.

Theological Science. New York: Oxford, 1969.

Theology in Reconciliation. London: Geoffrey Chapman, 1975.

The Ground and Grammar of Theology. Belfast: Christian Journals Limited, 1980.

Christian Theology and Scientific Culture. New York: Oxford, 1981.

Divine and Contingent Order. New York: Oxford, 1981.

Reality and Evangelical Theology. Philadelphia: Westminster, 1982.

The Mediation of Christ. Exeter: Paternoster, 1983.

Transformation and Convergence in the Frame of Knowledge: Explorations in the Interrelations of Scientific and Theological Enterprise. Grand Rapids: Eerdmans, 1984.

The Hermeneutics of John Calvin. Edinburgh: Scottish Academic Press, 1988.

The Trinitarian Faith. Edinburgh: T. and T. Clark, 1988.

The Christian Frame of Mind. Colorado Springs, Colo.: Helmers and Howard, 1989.

Karl Barth: Biblical and Evangelical Theologian. Edinburgh: T. and T. Clark, 1990.

$\mathcal{W}$hat do you consider the church's
most perfect creed or confession of faith, and
why do you think so?

The only creed I'd like to have is the Niceno-
Constantinopolitan Creed. It is strictly a creed. The con-
fessions are not creeds; they are, rather, constitutional
documents. Because it is the one creed upon which all
Christendom is based, the Niceno-Constantinopolitan
Creed is the only one we need. We need no others.

**What things have made you doubt, and how have you
handled them?**

I've never had any doubts. Why should I?

To me, the living God is the most real thing there is.
Knowledge of God is the most natural, most intuitive
thing of all, especially for me. I was raised in a Christian
home. My mother was a wonderfully pious woman, one
who was, in her own way, an excellent theologian. Belief
in God simply pervaded everything. To me, it has always
seemed so natural.

**What books and theologians have had the greatest
influence upon you?**

Athanasius and the Greek fathers are my love.
Athanasius' books are surely some of the greatest books

111

ever written. They combine spirituality and theology so wonderfully.

While I was a student in college, H. R. MacIntosh had an enormous effect on me. While I was a minister, it was Calvin to whom I repeatedly turned. His *Institutes* and his commentaries (especially his commentary on Hebrews) were in my hands continually.

Then, of course, there is Karl Barth, perhaps the most powerful theological mind we've had for many centuries. He was steeped in the Bible, and he was able to put things so clearly, ontologically and dynamically. He also had such a light-hearted godliness about him. I am persuaded that his *Doctrine of God* is simply the best thing of its kind.

What aspect of your thought do theologians continue to misunderstand?

Frankly, a lot of it.

I have tried to translate the message of the Bible and of the church fathers into a modern mode, into the world of modern culture, while being as faithful as possible to divine revelation. Like the ancient Christians, I have tried to translate Christianity into dynamic, not static, categories. But, I am afraid too many theologians continue to read me and interpret me according to their own (now outmoded) dualistic, or dichotomous, framework —that very framework the biblical gospel and Nicene theology destroy.

For example, too many theologians do not take the concepts of space and time properly or seriously as relational concepts. Nor do they appreciate pure science, which is our ally. With such things they often seem unconcerned and uninformed.

Too many theologians do not seem to understand what might be called "kinetic theology," which is dynamic and moving, not static. You see, I try to employ a kinetic mode of reason, without which I believe you simply cannot understand such things as God "becoming" flesh. Your thought must *move*, as it were. You must abandon theologizing from a point, or position, of absolute rest. A dynamic logic is required. Barth, I dare say, did this quite nicely. He held together both the being and the acts of God, both the ontological and the dynamic. I try to do the same, but it is neither well appreciated nor well understood.

Do you have any regrets?

Yes.

First, while I had the opportunity to lecture on various other important theological topics here in Edinburgh, I did not have the opportunity to lecture on the doctrine of God. To me, that was a great loss.

Second, Karl Barth very much wanted me to succeed him at Basel. In fact, the theology faculty asked me to do so. But, because my children would have had to switch from English to German in school, I did not. Had I gone to Basel, however, I probably would not have been able to develop the relationship between Christianity and science, at least not to the extent that it has been possible for me to do so in Britain.

Third, I regret that my scientific studies came so late in life. If I'd been younger, I might have had more time and done more. As it is, it took me fifteen years of hard work to repair that defect in my knowledge.

But, I *do not* regret my ten years in parish ministry, which enabled me to think *theologically*, and not pseudo-psychologically. Again and again I found that the fundamental theological questions were the very stuff of the deepest anxieties of the human heart, questions such as "Is God really like Jesus?" I discovered repeatedly that to minister effectively required a firm grasp of the gospel and of the theology of the incarnation, and not psychology.

**What is the role of the theologian in the church and in
the university?**

Within the church, the theologian (in the old Calvinist
sense of "doctor") must teach us to understand the
gospel *in terms of the gospel*. Therefore, he must be
steeped in the Scripture and in the gospel. He must
know how to interpret Scripture correctly, in terms of its
inner theological connections. This is far more than
mere grammatical exegesis.

In other words, the theologian has to do what the
ancient bishops often had to do in the early church.
They had to be, among other things, evangelists. The
theologian needs to help the church evangelize *the
entire culture*, not merely to snatch burning brands out
of the fire. Only a church that is theologically oriented
can do this.

The theologian also must help the church to resist secularization. He must divert the church from secularization back to Christ.

As for the university theologian, he must be a rigorous
and scientific thinker, one whose thought is guided by
the nature of the object he seeks to know.

He too, like the ecclesiastical theologian, must perform an evangelistic function. Only his job is to perform
the task of intellectual evangelization. I believe that in
my own career as a university theologian I have had to
be an intellectual evangelist both to scientists *and to
theologians.*

**What is the unfinished task of theology, and what
field of inquiry, or method of inquiry, seems
most promising to pursue now?**

Theology's task is not—and never can be—completed.
The current task of theologians is to think out the faith
within the divinely ordained universe disclosed through
scientific research. This is not to say that theology comes
from natural science or that natural science comes from
theology. But surely, they must be fully aware of, and

informed by, one another; and we must try to relate them to one another.

Additionally, the missionary enterprise is not yet completed. To advance it, we must resort to science, pure and applied, in order to help people respect the integrity of God's creation. You see, the countries of the Far East and of the Southern Hemisphere want our science and technology, but they have no doctrine of creation. They do not realize that science and technology rest upon, indeed arise from, Christian foundations. This is true both historically and epistemologically. We must show them that it is the Creator God himself who stands behind everything, and that he provides the rational ground upon which the various sciences rest, as well as the world those sciences unlock and help to tame. Theology and technology come as a pair. We must be quite firm about both this and their function in serving and respecting the integrity of nature.

What are the greatest problems facing those in your own religious tradition?

I have no question but that it is secularization, the same as it is in all the churches. By becoming inappropriately secularized (in order to be relevant), the church has made itself impotent. We need to be more thoroughly theological and evangelical, more faithful to the truth of the gospel.

Also, our seminaries are in a very low state, at the moment. They tend to produce ministers who can handle neither the gospel nor the modern world appropriately. They do not seem to acquire a genuine theological instinct.

What advice do you have for those of other religious traditions, especially American evangelicals?

I would advise them to take the evangelical and soteriological principles of the early church more seriously. That is, I would advise them, on the one hand, not to undervalue the homoousian doctrine, upon which everything hinges, and on the other hand, not to forget that Christ took upon himself our fallen humanity. But, in taking it upon himself, he redeemed and sanctified it. By God taking this upon himself, he was redeeming. You see, *the incarnation is already atoning,* and not merely his death. It is an atoning incarnation. The atonement is not separate from the incarnation. What is not assumed by God is not healed.

What is a human being?

A human being is the one creature God has made especially for communion and fellowship with himself. A human being is only fully a human being in his relationship to God. Detached from God, he is a monster. Detached from other humans, who are in the image of God, he is also a monster. That is because the concept of "human being" is a relational concept.

To put it another way, God has made us *personalized* persons, while he himself is the *personalizing* person or the *personalizer* of persons. Christ is the personalizer and humanizer of human persons.

Furthermore, we must realize this about human beings: when God became man, humanity and divinity became inseparably linked. When God became man, every person became *ontologically* related to God. Thus, when Christ died, we all died. When he rose from the dead, all men rose from the dead. He has exerted his effect upon the entire race and upon the entire universe. In the incarnation, the whole world was sanctified in him and turned around.

Describe God.

We can do that only from our Lord, Jesus Christ. He is, by his very nature, God.

What is the Christian gospel, and what is the best way to present it and defend it in the modern world?

The Christian gospel is the power of God to salvation. The gospel is Christ, who is Creator and Redeemer.

Union with him is the basis of our redemption and resurrection.

The gospel is a truly powerful, even devastating, reality. To believe it is to conquer sin and death. To reject it is to be crushed. These things I have seen with my own eyes.

What do you see as your greatest achievement, or the thing that gives you the most satisfaction?

The best thing I ever did was to get married and have a family.

It also has pleased me greatly to have been a minister of the gospel.

Theologically, I saw that everything was unfinished. I saw that we all need correction. Thus, I've tried to carry on the work of Athanasius and the ancients and of Calvin. But, I still see that it needs carrying on even yet.

Of my books, I am most pleased with *The Trinitarian Faith*.

I also have been fortunate to have been a part of bringing Karl Barth to English readers, and to work on this project with Geoffrey Bromiley, who is such a good theologian and translator.

How would you like to be remembered?

I would like to be remembered as someone who has been faithful to the gospel, both in his teaching and in his preaching.

What are the beauties and utilities of your theology, and what are its weaknesses and shortcomings?

Theology is a beautiful science. Its beauty comes from the beauty of God. If your theology is truly grounded in the living and beautiful God, it is a beautiful and effective theology. I believe that sort of beauty often happens in theology. But, it is very difficult to identify its presence with great precision in one's own theology.

My weakness, I think, is my style. I do not know a

way to put my theology across that makes for easy reading. Great minds like Einstein's and Barth's are able to
combine profundity with simplicity and intelligibility.

**What is a good life, and what good is life? What is a
good death, and what good is death?**

A good life is a life lived in union with and in enjoy-
ment of God in Christ, which is also what good life is.
Nothing is better or more worthwhile than that.

A good death is a death died in God. It then becomes a
gateway to the full presence of Christ, undimmed and
untarnished by the toil and darkness of this world.

**If you could ask any theologian of any time or place
just one question, who would you ask, and what
would you ask?**

You are asking me what I would ask Athanasius; what
I would ask John Calvin; and what I would ask Karl
Barth.

I think I'd press Athanasius for deeper specification
about the doctrine of the Trinity, and about the relation
of the Trinity to spirituality, indeed to the whole of creation.

I'd ask Calvin about his view of the humanity and
divinity of Christ, about his view of the episcopate in the
church, and about his understanding of world missions.

I'd ask Karl Barth about the element of subordination-
ism in his theology, and about how he understood the
obedience of Christ to the will of the Father.

10

Alister E. McGrath
Oxford, England

Reverend Dr. Alister E. McGrath is currently lecturer in historical and systematic theology at Wycliffe Hall, Oxford, where he has been since 1983. He is also a member of the theological faculty of Oxford University. Previously, he was curate of Saint Leonard's Church, Wollaton.

Dr. McGrath earned a B.A. in natural sciences and a D.Phil. in molecular biophysics, as well as a B.A., M.A. and B.D. in theology, all from Oxford University.

He is currently at work as the general editor of the forthcoming *Blackwell Encyclopedia of Modern Christian Thought,* as well as on an introduction to systematic theology for seminary students and a critique of liberal Christian theology. His current work also includes research centering upon John Calvin and Joachim von Watt.

Dr. McGrath was the Oxford University Bampton Lecturer for 1990.

Select Bibliography

Luther's Theology of the Cross. Oxford: Basil Blackwell, 1985.

Iustitia Dei: A History of the Christian Doctrine of Justification. 2 vols. Cambridge: Cambridge University Press, 1986.

The Making of Modern German Christology: From the Enlightenment to Pannenberg. Oxford: Basil Blackwell, 1986.

The Intellectual Origins of the European Reformation. Oxford: Basil Blackwell, 1987.

The Mystery of the Cross. Grand Rapids: Zondervan, Academie Books, 1988.

Reformation Thought: An Introduction. Oxford: Basil Blackwell, 1988.

The Genesis of Doctrine. Oxford: Basil Blackwell, 1990.

A Life of John Calvin. Oxford: Basil Blackwell, 1990.

What do you consider the church's most perfect creed or confession of faith, and why do you think so?

While I do appreciate the more recent confessions like the Augsburg Confession or the Heidelberg Catechism, I think the finest creed of all is the Apostles' Creed. I think so because it is fully developable into a complete theology; because it is simple while yet containing the main outlines of Christian belief; and because it is easily memorizable, which makes it ideal both for teaching and for learning.

What things have made you doubt, and how have you handled them?

The main difficulty that I have is the apparent tension between faith and experience. God often does not seem to be there. In the agonies of life, in the suffering of the Third World, or in the crush of the cities, God often does not seem present. There is a big question mark here.

That is one of the reasons why I like Martin Luther as a theologian. He actually addresses this problem. What we have to learn is that God acts in a way that is not often immediately obvious to us; and that what seems to be God's absence is really God's hidden presence. This is where Luther's concept of the hidden God, or *Deus absconditus*, comes in.

Additionally, one needs to learn that (as Tennyson wrote in *The Ancient Sage*) nothing worthwhile can be proved: not Christianity, not any political theory, and not any ethical philosophy. That is because such things go beyond the senses. But, as I say, this is not simply a Christian difficulty. It is one shared by anything worthy.

What books and theologians have had the greatest influence upon you?

Martin Luther, of course, comes to mind first. He was a pastor and a spiritual writer, and not merely an academic theologian. He was so very practical. The *Heidelberg Disputation* is the writing that perhaps has influenced me most.

Then, of course, there is C. S. Lewis. His sermon, "The Weight of Glory," is one in which he puts his finger on so many important ideas. His *Miracles,* furthermore, is perhaps the best thing of its kind, and has never been bettered.

To speak more generally, I have been impressed by the seriousness of the German theological tradition. It is much more systematic than our English tradition, which is more sporadic; which lacks a well-defined system or school of thought; and which lacks any acknowledged masters. From the German-speaking tradition, Karl Barth has been most helpful to me.

What aspect of your thought do theologians continue to misunderstand?

I don't think I am yet well enough known to be widely misunderstood. But, I *expect* many will misunderstand (or stridently dissent from) my soon-to-be published Bampton Lectures, which will be entitled *The Genesis of Doctrine.* In it, I contend that theology can be done and understood only from inside the believing tradition. It cannot be adequately evaluated by anybody outside the Christian community. This principle also holds true, to a large extent, even within the Christian tradition. Liberals, for example, cannot understand or appreciate conservatism while they yet remain outside of it.

Do you have any regrets?

I wish I had started doing theology when I was younger. My first degree and my doctorate are in the natural sciences, which means I was twenty-five before I started studying theology seriously. Had I started earlier, say at age eighteen, I might be a better theologian.

Nevertheless, my scientific training has helped me to integrate my Christian faith with a scientific world view and to make some useful connections in that regard.

What is the role of the theologian in the church and in the university?

The theologian has both a positive and a critical role.

His positive function is to try to articulate and defend the Christian proclamation to his own day and age. He must learn to contextualize the gospel effectively. His critical function, by comparison, is to say what is right *and wrong* with our way of thinking and of acting. But, he should do this responsibly, as one under authority, an authority that goes all the way back to the Bible and to Christ himself. The theologian cannot start all over again. He cannot produce the gospel *de novo,* so to speak. He works from within a tradition, and that tradition exerts an influence upon him that he needs to deal with properly. He must resist the temptation of the Enlightenment to separate himself from his tradition and to begin again.

Within the university, one quickly sees that academic theology has become increasingly marginalized. At a university where financial considerations loom large, a theologian can seem an irrelevant and unnecessary academic luxury. Theology seems a mere holdover from an earlier, now outmoded, period of history. The modern academic theologian, as a university creature, is under threat.

What is the unfinished task of theology, and what field of inquiry, or method of inquiry, seems best to pursue now?

It seems to me that one very exciting line of inquiry would be to explore the methods and modes of representation in the natural sciences and in theology and to relate them to one another. We might discover that we have a great deal in common. This would serve as a means of mutual clarification and lead perhaps to a better Christian apologetic.

What are the greatest problems facing those in your own religious tradition?

First, in England, Christianity is not taken seriously, which is demoralizing to theologians. We must ask ourselves the apologetic and evangelistic question: "How do you raise the profile of Christianity?"

Second, English Christianity suffers from the absence of a serious theological tradition. Because we do, we lack the resultant sense that a given body of theologians (and their church) actually *belong together.*

What advice do you have for those of other traditions, especially American evangelicals?

Some modern American evangelicals do seem very anti-intellectual. I'd like to see a greater academic awareness on the part of some. They are hot on piety and politics, but on matters of theology they sometimes seem unnecessarily hostile to critical exploration of the Christian faith. For me, Christianity is perfectly capable of standing up to such investigation.

What is a human being?

A human being is a being who has been created by God and who has the possibility now of being re-created, or renewed, in the image and likeness of God.

The important thing is the inherent capacity of human beings to relate to God, which the proclamation of the gospel brings. God addresses us in the gospel and is able to elicit a response from us. Though this is not all we are, it is certainly a high point.

Describe God.

The best description of God is the God-given self-revelation in Jesus Christ. This is why for me the best definition of God is "the one we encounter through Jesus Christ."

God is the one who stands behind and who raised up Jesus Christ. He is the one whom Jesus reveals.

You see, the New Testament identifies God by looking at Jesus. That is why the best place to look for God is in the New Testament pictures of Christ.

What is the Christian gospel, and what is the best way to present it and to defend it in the modern world?

The Christian gospel arises from the fact that Jesus is Lord, and it entails all the implications of that great fact. The gospel follows out those implications for our lives, our church, and our world.

The best way to present it is to refuse to capitulate to the world. Never water down the gospel. It does not work to try it. We must not reduce the gospel to the world. Instead, we must be faithful to the gospel as it is.

What do you see as your greatest achievement, or the thing that gives you the most satisfaction?

I am moved by getting letters that say "What you wrote in your book really helped me." Such letters let me know that God is using me. That is both profoundly satisfying and profoundly humbling.

How would you like to be remembered?

I would like to be remembered as someone who presented Christianity and its credentials to a world puzzled by them. I'd like to have helped remove some of the barriers to faith.

**What are the beauties and utilities of your theology,
and what are its weaknesses and shortcomings?**

English theology has the advantages that arise from
preaching, from the liturgy and the liturgical year (and
all the regularity and scope that entails), and of the communion service.

But, English theology includes a great deal of dissatis-
faction with authority. We have not yet figured out how
bishops and Bibles relate to each other. It is all still
unclear.

**What is a good life, and what good is life? What is a
good death, and what good is death?**

Regarding a good life, I think of what George Herbert
once wrote: "For that which God doth touch and own
cannot for less be told." That is, the life God touches is a
good life. In fact, life *begins* with the touch of God.

As to what good is life, I can think of various answers,
though I'm not sure any are very good. But I can say this:
God does not give us things without there being a good
purpose. All his gifts are given with a purpose in mind.
I'm just happy that God has given me life, and that he
intends me to use it. I *do* want to use it. You see, God
gave me my life, and I want to give it as a gift back to
him.

A good death is one's final act of Christian witness,
especially insofar as the way one dies reflects the way
one lives. A good death, in other words, is one in which
the presence and nearness of God shine through.

The good of death is that, after Christ, we die in hope.
That means that after death, *all the barriers are removed.*

**If you could ask any theologian of any time or place
just one question, whom would you ask and what
would you ask?**

In light of recent events, I'd like to ask A. J. Ayer,
"Have you changed your mind?"

11

John Macquarrie
Oxford, England

John Macquarrie earned an M.A., B.D., Ph.D., and D.Litt. from the University of Glasgow, as well as an M.A. and D.D. from the University of Oxford. In addition to these, he has received honorary doctorates from a half-dozen schools both in America and the United Kingdom, among them the University of the South, General Theological Seminary, Virginia Theological Seminary, and Nashota House.

Dr. Macquarrie was the Lady Margaret Professor of Divinity at the University of Oxford from 1970 to 1986. Previously he had been a member of the theological faculties of the University of Glasgow and Union Theological Seminary. He was also Canon of Christ Church, Oxford, and is a Fellow of the British Academy.

Professor Macquarrie has recently completed work on two books: *Jesus Christ in Modern Thought* and *Mary for All Christians*.

Select Bibliography

An Existentialist Theology: A Comparison of Heidegger and Bultmann. London: SCM, 1955.

Principles of Christian Theology. New York: Scribner, 1966/1977.

The Concept of Peace. London: SCM, 1973.

Christian Hope. New York: Seabury, 1978.

Twentieth-Century Religious Thought. New York: Scribner, 1981.

In Search of Humanity. New York: Crossroad, 1985.

In Search of Deity. New York: Crossroad, 1987.

What do you consider the church's most perfect creed or confession of faith, and why do you think so?

I believe it is the Niceno-Constantinopolitan Creed of 381. I think so because it is reasonably detailed. That is, it touches on all the main issues. Yet, it is not so detailed as to prevent theological variety and development. It also is perhaps the most ecumenical document in the Christian church. Nearly all churches that use creeds use it in their liturgy.

This is not to say, however, that the language of the creed is not difficult, even obsolete. This means that we must educate the people to its content, not rewrite it. We must expound and explain it.

What things have made you doubt, and how have you handled them?

A great many things can cause doubt.

My first degree was in philosophy. To study philosophy raises a great many questions. One is forced to formulate reasons and grounds for religious beliefs.

Even more than that, the age in which we live makes religious belief difficult. The current of the time is secularistic, and I find myself always working against that current. Thus, in the face of this onslaught, unless one is unduly dogmatic one must inwardly ask serious questions. As a result, one experiences doubts.

As times goes on, however, I become more convinced of the truth of the Christian faith.

What books and theologians have had the greatest influence upon you?

At different stages in one's life, different writers play the most prominent role.

When I was a student of philosophy, F. H. Bradley, the English idealist, prevented me from embracing modern theologians (like Karl Barth) whom, though I can appreciate them, I cannot fully accept.

After seminary, I acquired a distaste for theology. Perhaps I had had too much. I then turned away from theology—though not from Christianity. When I returned, I took up the theology of Rudolf Bultmann very enthusiastically.

What aspect of your thought do theologians continue to misunderstand?

Whenever one writes or says anything, there is a danger of misunderstanding. At times you almost despair; you think that you have spoken clearly, but you realize you have not.

At the moment, however, I cannot identify anything particular that persistently gives rise to misunderstanding.

Do you have any regrets?

Yes, I regret the period of time I turned away from theology. If you give yourself to any subject, you must give yourself to it completely.

I also regret not reading the books and writers I missed. There are some I wish I knew much more about. For example, the patristic period is something I wish I knew better than I do. Eastern Orthodoxy is another.

What is the role of the theologian in the church and in the university?

This is a difficult and delicate question.

I see the role of the theologian in the church as that of adviser and of critic. The theologian, you see, has a degree of freedom that a bishop does not. This independence allows them to experiment, and to get into trouble!

Nevertheless, the theologian is a member of the Christian community. He is not a "free-lance" thinker. He speaks within (and from) the church. But, this church he also needs to prod occasionally.

I must say here that the church does not always make good use of its theologians. Theologians can do great service as consultants, for example, as Origen did centuries ago. This would be good both for the theologian and the church.

Tensions arise for theologians within the university as well. Since the Enlightenment, universities everywhere have become increasingly secularized and dominated by the sciences. Where theological faculties still exist, they have become quite isolated. In such settings, the theologians must display academic integrity. In doing so, we must resist the temptation to "lay down the law" on subjects outside our strict purview (such as science or history). We need to avoid glib generalizations.

What is the unfinished task of theology, and what field of inquiry, or method of inquiry, seems best to pursue now?

The task of theology will never be finished. Christian theology has always been developing—and even retrogressing! Short of the vision of God we are presented hereafter, it never will be finished.

I am convinced that we now must turn our attention to the question of God, which needs thought. "Where and how do we find God in the world of physics?" and

"Who is Jesus Christ?" are examples of the sort of questions to which we need to address ourselves.

What are the greatest problems facing those in your own religious tradition?

I would say that the greatest problem facing the Church of England is the same problem one finds everywhere in Western Europe: entire sections of the population simply do not care about Christianity. We face massive indifference. Out of a nation of over fifty million, something less than two million have an active relationship with, or role within, the church.

What advice do you have for those of other traditions, especially American evangelicals?

I am not one that is keen on seeing all the churches coming together into a single body. I think there has to be variety. In America, you have enough churches that almost anyone can find a home for their faith. So I advise Americans to preserve your traditions and continue to offer the variety you do. Maintain your theological diversity. In so doing, you will better serve the needs of your very diverse country.

What is a human being?

What I think is distinctive in the human being is summarized in the two words *freedom* and *transcendence*. Freedom is our choice to be one thing or another. To some extent, a human being makes himself or herself. Humans are not ready-made. They have possibilities. That leads to the closely related concept of transcendence. We not only have possibilities, we have the capacity, indeed the desire, to reach out to what it is we might be or could be.

Yet, we too often forget our finitude and (even more) our sinfulness. If I were to rewrite my book on humanity, I would put greater emphasis on the dark side of human nature, especially aggression and acquisitiveness.

Describe God.

I'm afraid I can't describe God.

God retreats in the face of definition. The more we try to pin him down, the more elusive he becomes.

Having said that, however, I do believe we have made our view of God improperly "exalted," so to speak. By that I mean that we have unduly exaggerated his sovereignty, and his transcendence. We have made him the "Louis XIV of heaven." I feel that part of my task in my later years will be to teach *the humility of God.* Surely he is sovereign, but he is also self-giving and vulnerable, because he is love. He shares our life. He has even taken death into himself. He has not been content to dwell in undisturbed bliss.

What is the Christian gospel, and what is the most effective way to present it and defend it in the modern world?

That would take a book to answer, and I'm not sure I would be the person to write it.

But let me answer you this way. To put it at the lowest level, the Christian gospel says that there is hope and meaning in human life.

The gospel needs to be put at the lowest level. It needs to be stated in a low-key fashion. You'll notice that I did not mention God or Jesus Christ at all. That is because we must begin with the human predicament and then rise to the contemplation of what God has done in Christ on our behalf.

What do you see as your greatest achievement, or the one that gives you the most satisfaction?

I am most pleased with my *Principles of Christian Theology* because it has been used in seminaries all over the world. Nowadays it is even used in Nanking, in Communist China. It pleases me to know I have helped people to understand Christianity. I hope I have not misled them too much.

How would you like to be remembered?

I haven't really thought of that. So long as I'm still around, I won't worry about how I'll be remembered!

What are the beauties and utilities of your theology, and what are its weaknesses and shortcomings?

In a way, I can't really answer this question. I can only say what I've tried to do: I've tried to address my theology to people's existential situation. I've tried to address where we are going, and what we shall become.

Like all theologians, however, I do think that there are large areas about which I simply do not know enough. I wonder, too, if I have not been blind about the dark side of human life, and not sufficiently challenged by it.

What is a good life, and what good is life? What is a good death, and what good is death?

A good life is one which proves satisfactory to the one living it. A good life is one that affords opportunities for growth. It is one that is helpful to other people, and is thus unselfish. That is also something of an indication of what a good life is.

A good death "rounds off" a good life (rather than, let us say, a death that cuts down a young life in mid-career).

We must learn to live in the expectation of death. We must learn that we are finite. We must fulfill our vocation. Death reminds us that there is a cut-off point. Without this sense of termination, we'd become lazy and aimless. Death provides urgency.

If you could ask any theologian of any time or place just one question, whom would you ask and what would you ask?

I can't really say. I honestly have no burning desire to ask someone (let us say Thomas Aquinas) a probing question. I just don't know.

A Concluding Evangelical Postscript

Scientists long have known that the scientist inescapably has an effect upon his experiments. None of his data are pristine. While his conclusions may not be false, neither are they untainted.

That discovery, to many scientists, proved a bitter pill. It was unsettling and unnerving because it called into question the very nature of scientific knowledge itself. But it was, nevertheless, a beneficial and academically therapeutic discovery. It helped prepare the way back from an unduly dogmatic scientism to a more healthy skepticism of (and appreciation for) just what it is that scientists can do and have done. That same humbling lesson is one that we theologians ought to learn about ourselves.

The theologians whose viewpoints make up the bulk of this book are all mature, well-educated, well-intentioned, intelligent, pious, productive thinkers who work from a position inside the church. They all believe Christianity is true and that it comes from God. They have committed not only their careers to the faith, but their own final destinies as well. But that commitment does not produce theological uniformity. On some very significant points they do not agree—theology proper, anthropology, ecclesiology, soteriology, spirituality, and politics to name a few.

They disagree because, like we American evangelicals, they are not untouched by imperfect learning and perception, skewed perspective, faulty synthesis, or sin.

Thus, while reason itself might remain reliable, indeed inviolable, their own—and our own—portion of it does not. We all are subject to theological failure, especially to the failure of not knowing where we have failed. That is because theology is not a heavenly enterprise; it is a human one.

Theology, like science, is not free from the taint of those who practice it. Like all else to which we put our hands, theology "wears man's smudge and shares man's smell." Like it or not, theology is a human endeavor, and we all probably need to distinguish more carefully and more humbly between what the Bible teaches and what is taught by theologians. While those two categories ought ideally to be the same, the plain fact is that they are not.

What I am saying is this: while the perspicuity of the Scriptures and the illumination by the Holy Spirit are real, they clearly have not combined to prevent what simply must be widespread error. Because we live in a world where truth is singular and where two opposite things cannot both be correct, and because we find ourselves occupying but one point among many along a wide-ranging theological spectrum, we know that not all the beliefs held on any one issue of Christian doctrine can be appropriate, much less can all systems of doctrine. Nor can we safely assume that all the error, or even the bulk of that error, must lie outside our camp. Perhaps it does; but that is not obvious. We must remember that Jesus's promise that the Spirit would guide them into all truth was given to his immediate disciples, not to the Eastern Orthodox, the Roman Catholics, the German Lutherans, the Anglicans, the Dutch Reformed, or the American evangelicals. To paraphrase something said earlier in these pages by Gareth Moore, while there are many human theologies, there is no privileged human theology. We must avoid the attitude that turns our beliefs into facts and our theology into revelation.

After the Delphic oracle told Socrates that he was the

wisest of men, Socrates reacted with surprise. "Who, me?" he wondered. "I don't know much at all!" But as he pondered further, he realized that, in fact, the oracle was correct. While we humans all are ignorant and uninformed, at least Socrates knew it. Most of us are ignorant even of our ignorance. For us, as for Socrates, the path to wisdom probably leads close by Delphi. We have a lesson to learn.

We should also learn from earlier Christians like Erasmus and Melanchthon, who realized in a way that Luther never could, that the peripherals are many and the essentials are few. Those essentials are summed up best, Erasmus thought, in something like the Apostles' Creed. This fact helped give rise to Melanchthon's admirable aphorism: "In things essential, unity; in things not essential, liberty; in all things, charity."

In short, I am pleading here on behalf of what I have pleaded for elsewhere: teachableness and the cessation of unproductive inter-camp (even intra-camp) warfare. I am advocating a consentual pluralism, not relativism.

Hold what you hold with conviction. But hold it humbly and teachably. There is a right answer; but on some questions we just don't know for sure who but God has it.

Appendix

In order to answer questions that I anticipate might arise in the reader's mind about how these interviews were arranged and about how this book was assembled, the following paragraphs will be useful.

First, because I was not then personally acquainted with the theologians to whom I wished to speak, and because I did not want to presume upon their good will, I assured my interviewees of my irenic intentions in my initial contact with them. My purpose, they were told, was the wider dissemination of theological wisdom, not an extension of interfactional sniping. I also enclosed for their examination a copy of the questions that I intended to ask them. I informed them of the dates I would be in Europe and asked them to select what for them would be a convenient time and place for our interview. They did; and except for Richard Holloway, the Bishop of Edinburgh (who, ironically, was scheduled to be in the U.S. while I was scheduled to be in Scotland), their stated preferences were for the most part readily accommodated. The arrangements with Father Gareth Moore and Sister Benedicta Ward, however, were made only at the last minute. To the credit of both those fine people, they graciously allowed me to interrupt their work and agreed to answer without any preparation the difficult questions of a complete stranger.

Second, in order to set my interviewees at ease, before our conversations began I promised to each one that he or she would have the opportunity to examine and, if necessary, to amend or correct the printed text of the interview prior to publication. In this way, nothing inaccurate or embarrassing (either to them or to me) would be put into print. This promise I have gladly kept. Thus, the conversations that appear in these pages do so with the express approval of those whose words they are. The same is true for the select bibliography that precedes each interview.

Subject Index

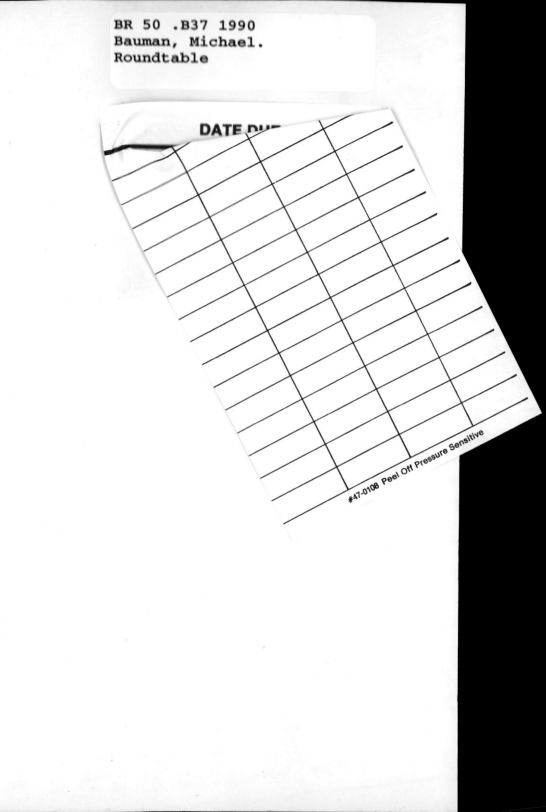

DATE DUE

#47-0108 Peel Off Pressure Sensitive